THE COMPLETE GUIDE TO HOME
WINEMAKING

THE COMPLETE GUIDE TO HOME WINEMAKING

BRIAN LEVERETT
M.Phil. Ph.D
Member of the National Guild of Wine and Beer Judges

PRISM PRESS

Dedication: To Sheila

Originally published in 1995 by
PRISM PRESS
The Thatched Cottage
Partway Lane
Hazelbury Bryan
Sturminster Newton
Dorset DT10 2DP
Great Britain.

Distributed in the USA by
ASSOCIATED PUBLISHERS GROUP
Nashville, TN 37218, U.S.A.

ISBN 1 85327 099 7

Cover artwork: Myra Giles

Made and printed in Great Britain by the
Guernsey Press Co. Ltd., Guernsey, Channel Islands

CONTENTS

AUTHOR'S FOREWORD

It is now fifty years since home winemaking re-emerged after the end of the second world war and part of the home economy, which had remained virtually unaltered for three centuries, gradually began to change. It evolved only slowly at first. In the early days we still relied very heavily on the old traditional methods, with recipes which had stood the test of time, in many cases because no one had bothered to challenge them.

Here was a way to legally avoid excise duty and it caught the imagination. Soon everyone seemed to be making wines at home, wine circles sprung up and homebrew shops appeared in most towns. Home winemaking was the in thing to do. Products appeared on the market which claimed to make the operation easier, to produce wines in a far shorter time, often accompanied by that universal marketing ploy that they were cheaper than their competitors. Most of these products have long since disappeared, but amongst them there were quality products which did what they claimed and these have lead to better winemaking.

But times were changing, the very thing which was the appeal of home winemaking - the differential between the price of the home prepared product and its bought equivalent - was narrowing as the various taxes on wine were coming closer into line with the more favourable situation in continental Europe. The amount of 'duty free' wine which you were allowed to bring into the country rose and home winemaking began to lose some of its appeal. But only for a short time, for it was soon realised that whilst the cheaper end of the market is certainly more affordable, quality wines, especially the well made dessert styles such as ports, still command very high prices outside of most people's budget. In addition, homemade wines still hold a depth of character seldom reached in the commercial equivalents, and they provide a range of drinks far greater than that which can be obtained from using grapes alone.

For years home winemakers looked to the commercial field for knowledge, they imitated their practices and sought to use similar products, but now in one respect the tables have been reversed. 'Country wines' are now widely produced and sold throughout the country relying on ingredients and methods developed by the home winemaker. Such wines are often more expensive than many cheaper wines made solely from grapes. The commercial production and the acceptance of such drinks recognises the demand for the variety that country wines provide and the quality which can be reached. And comparing like with like all of this you can still achieve for yourself at a fraction of the cost. Making your own wine holds one other big advantage - by blending you can make a drink designed exactly to suit your individual palate.

In the past winemaking was fruit centred with recipes designed to utilise any spare fruit available, quality was a secondary consideration - part of the old 'Waste not want not' philosophy. Modern winemaking has moved on to a wine centred approach in which recipes and methods have been formulated to produce the best drinks possible. *The Complete Guide to Home Wine Making* is concerned solely with the production of top quality wines and the limited number of basic recipes which allow you to make those drinks. Consequently I have discarded many of the traditional ingredients, flowers such as dandelion, gorse and broom add very little to a wine. The only way in which they alter the base wine is to provide a slight flavour of the decaying greenery. In spite of several years trying of no one has successfully made a beetroot wine which would appeal to present day tastes. This and wines like it are also omitted.

The recipes are written in such away as to be self contained although there is a degree of cross referencing to avoid unnecessary repetition. However it cannot be stressed too strongly that the theory and longer discussion contained in the first part of the book is an integral and important part of the art and skill of the winemaker which the reader is recommended strongly to study and to use it as a launch pad from which to make the very best wines.

BRIAN LEVERETT
Poole, Dorset
1995

1: INTRODUCTION

WHY MAKE WINES?

At a time when bought wine is cheaper in real terms than it has ever been, the first question which anyone contemplating winemaking may justifiably ask is 'why bother to make wine?'. Surely the argument used in the past, economy, no longer applies. With cheap drinks available for purchase, why spend time and effort brewing your own when you can go down to the supermarket or off-licence and buy them at an affordable price? This is true - you can buy wines at very reasonable prices, but even the cheapest are unlikely to compete costwise with the homemade product. And what about the quality? The most expensive wines are superior to our homemade efforts but this is not necessarily true at the bottom end or even the middle of the market. Many cheap red wines, due to their method of manufacture and their all too short maturation times, tend to be far too high in tannin, quickly drying out the mouth and leaving a lingering astringency around the teeth and gums. Amongst the sweet reds quality is expensive. Cheap sweet reds are often very poor seconds, tending to cloy and lacking the body and depth of character that this type of wine demands. Good ports are superb but their price remains out of reach for most of us except for special occasions. But when the home winemaker starts to work on blackberries, elderberries and damsons a whole new range of drinks of real quality can be produced. White wines have always been more difficult but there are ingredients - gooseberries, apples, rhubarb, white currants, peaches, plums and bananas - which put these within our grasp.

Perhaps the only limitation on the quality of homemade wines lies in our understanding of the subject - the more we know the better our products. Modern homemade wines are far superior to those of the past and one day we may be able to surpass the very best of the bought wines. There is no sound scientific reason why wines made from grapes by professional vintners should be better than those made at home from a limitless choice of ingredients. Logic suggests that the opposite is probably true.

WHY IS WINEMAKING THEORY NECESSARY?

The second question is 'why bother with understanding winemaking theory when all that is required is a good recipe?'.

Yes, it is possible to make very acceptable wines relying solely on recipes in books such as *Winemaking Month By Month*, and for most people this has been the way into the hobby. Yet however good any recipe is, it has its limitations. At best it restricts you to using exact amounts of specified ingredients and it makes no allowance for the differences between the varieties of a particular type of fruit. Gooseberries make white wine, but if you use the

14

widely grown variety 'Whinham's Industry', with its hairy red berries, the resultant wine is a rosé. This is an extreme example; often the differences are far more subtle but just as relevant. Some varieties are sweeter than others, some more acidic, and some have completely different flavours.

Seeking the best from your homemade wine means you must be able to recognise these differences and turn them to your advantage. Usually the most effective way of doing this is by blending, so that the finished wine is tailored to your requirements. Many winemakers produce standard wines which change imperceptibly over many years simply by the skilful way that they blend.

WHAT IS WINE?

The third question that the would-be winemaker must ask is 'What is this thing called wine?'. Wine for sale has a strict legal definition applied to it, with restrictions on what can be used in its manufacture, even where the grapes are grown in order to comply with the labelling regulations. This book is concerned solely with wines made in the home for consumption by the people who made them. The term wine is used in a strictly generic sense to describe those alcoholic drinks of higher strength than beers and ciders. The other commonly used term to describe the drinks are country wines.

THE ELEMENTS OF WINE

Let us look at wine and break it down into its component parts.

Wine is a complex mixture of tastes and flavours which impart their unique character on the liquid. In order to understand how to make quality drinks, it is necessary to appreciate these factors and see how we can influence their presence in the final drink.

The achievement of maximum enjoyment from wine is a total experience. Great wines, whether homemade or bought, are works of art and should be appreciated as such. Whenever you drink wine you should be analysing it, mentally dissecting it, attempting to detect and understand its nuances. In this way you will not only be improving your appreciation of wine, which in itself enables you to make better drinks, but the extra knowledge obtained will increase your enjoyment. Everyone drinks some commercial wines and, whenever you do, you should make a special effort to learn something from them. But be warned, they may not necessarily be better than the homemade equivalents, especially if you are drinking the cheaper plonks.

The main features of wine are:

Alcohol

The alcohol or spirit referred to in wine is ethyl alcohol (ethanol). Occasionally the so-called higher alcohols or fusel oils may be found in country wines such as 'Carrot Whisky' and tend to be very harsh to the taste. They will leave you with a bad head should you drink a large amount. Fortunately these higher alcohols tend to be uncommon and need not concern us further.

Alcohol is detected by a burning sensation at the back of the mouth, with high alcohol wines it is possible to suck the air from across the top of the wine and detect its presence at the back of the throat. The intensity of burning is a rough guide to the alcohol level, and with experience this can be extremely useful in assessing the strength of a wine. Alcohol, as well as bestowing vinosity or winelike character on the drink, acts as a preservative. In concentrations above 12 -13% infection by organisms is unlikely. Whilst alcohol is a very important component of a wine it is wrong to think that it is the most important, and you should not seek to increase its concentration for its own sake. Low bodied table wines which are high in alcohol tend to be harsh, unpleasant drinks.

Sweetness

A wine which displays the characteristic of excess sugar is described as sweet, one with no discernable sweetness as dry. There are many different levels of sweetness between these two extremes and it is necessary to understand what is meant by the terms medium dry - where the wine is predominantly dry but there is a just faint discernable trace of sweetness, medium which as the name implies is intermediate between sweet and dry wine and medium sweet which is intermediate between medium and sweet - definitely sweet but lacking the sugar of a fully sweet wine. The only way to really appreciate the difference between the various degrees of sweetness is to taste some well known sweet and dry wines. An example of a real dry wine in the commercial field is a Muscadet - note the complete absence of any sensation of sweetness. Good examples of sweet wines include port or Sauternes. These wines are sweet but the sugar does not dominate, nor is it the over-riding feature but seems totally natural, an indispensable and inseparable component of the drink. As well as the increased body resulting from the extra fruit in a dessert wine the sugar itself gives weight to the wine. Many shops include a description and an indication by means of a scale as to the degree of sweetness and dryness. When tasting such bought wines always seek to first independently assess the sweetness and compare with the data provided.

Sweetness in country wines may be due to either unfermented sugars, or added non sugar sweeteners such as saccharin. Whilst creation of true sweet wines presents few problems as they invariably require high alcohol levels, wines with limited sweetness, usually associated with lower strength drinks, tend to be less predictable as most will referment. If such wines are left long enough they will usually work down to a dry drinks.

Astringency
This is the bite which a wine contains, it is the robustness that lifts it from a fruit cordial. Astringency is due to the presence of tannin, acid and alcohol. Each makes its own contribution and all three must be present in the correct amounts for the wine to enliven the mouth. Where any one of the factors is present in excess the wine is harsh.

Tannin
Tannin gives the wine zest - it is detected on the gums and around the cheeks. If you are not familiar with the sensation of tannin taste a cup of tea without milk or sugar. It is the astringency which you experience in your mouth that is the characteristic sensation of tannin. The amount of tannin is critical, insufficient and the wine is bland, lifeless; too much and the wine is far too astringent, verging

on the undrinkable.

There are many different tannins - all related to tannic acid, a phenol. Tannins are found in leaves, on the skins of fruit, and in the seeds and pips. It is the quantity of tannin more than any other single characteristic which distinguishes between the tastes of red, rosé and white commercial grape wines. Since red wines are made by fermenting the juice on the skins for a week or longer this will dissolve out the tannin, which in a pure form is colourless. As the level of alcohol increases larger amounts of both pigment and tannin will be removed from the skins. With commercial wines the deeper the colour the higher the level of tannin. But pigment and tannin are different and it does not necessarily follow that just because a fruit has a deep pigment it will automatically have a high tannin level. Some fruits, blackberries and elderberries, unlike grapes, have deep red juices. These can be extracted complete with their colour leaving the astringent tannin behind. Elderberries fermented on the skins for a week will produce a drink so rich in tannin that it will take several years to become sufficiently mellow to drink. But if you extract the juice by a press or other means and use this, without the skins, to make the wine it is no longer harsh whilst young. The use of such fruits provide the country wine maker with far greater scope for manipulation compared to the commercial vigneron tied to just grapes.

Tannin has a very important secondary role - that of clearing a wine. It combines to form a complex with protein materials in the liquid, the large molecules formed gradually fall out of solution clearing the liquid in the process. It is not mere coincidence that wines made from good well balanced recipes clear without problems. Egg white, gelatin and the other organic clearing agents all react with the tannin in the wine to form large mesh-like molecules which will trap any colloidal material. Where none of the simple clearing methods work it is usually the result of the wine containing insufficient tannin - a fact that can be easily demonstrated. Often, if you have a wine that will not clear, the addition of a small quantity of tannin, and standing the wine out of doors on a cold night, will be sufficient to produce a heavy colloidal precipitate. The dark stains which develop on the sides of demijohns and bottles are complexes consisting of tannin and pigment molecules bonded together. Should you ever make a wine that does not clear, it may be due to a variety of reasons and you must establish the cause - either the recipe or the technique is incorrect. Unless you identify the reason for the trouble and rectify it, it will only reoccur in successive brews. Continual use of fining agents is not the way to deal with clearing problems.

The importance of tannin to the winemaking process has been appreciated since the first country wines were made. Oak leaf and tea wines were much respected by the old winemakers. All that these two ingredients provide is tannin, but it was soon realised that such wines had zest and they always cleared - two characteristics often missing from traditional country wines.

The amount of tannin differs considerably between varieties of the same fruit, apple juice from dessert varieties may contain as little as 0.05% tannin whereas in cider apples it can be as high as 0.25% by weight. Taste an apple wine that does not clear and in most instances you will find that it lacks zest due to its tannin deficiency.

Where this has been a problem in the past the winemaker is advised to include extra tannin at the initial fermentation stage. Similar, although not as pronounced, variations occur with varieties of other fruit. Unfortunately, there is no simple chemical test for tannins. You will need to acquire an awareness of the taste sensation through drinking a range of wines.

There are a variety of ways in which you can provide the necessary tannin. Some fruits will possess sufficient, some even too much. The old country wine method was to add a cup of cold tea. Hit and miss, but it can be used satisfactorily if you know your ingredients. Grape tannin, either as a powder or a solution, is far better. Dried fruit, especially raisins, will often provide sufficient tannin without further additions. One special type of tannin is found in oak, which the alcohol will gradually leach out of barrels to give that special feature - oakiness. Much sort after in certain types of wine, it can be deliberately added in the form of oak chips to give the impression of barrel maturation.

Acidity

Acid gives the wine a sharp, sour taste. As well as its contribution to the character of the drink, it has important roles to perform in the actual winemaking process. Without sufficient acid the wine acquires a medicinal taste because the yeast is less efficient during fermentation and side reactions result in undesirable byproducts. Acid is an important component of esters, whose formation are essential to the maturation and mellowing of the wine and whose presence reduce the dangers of bacterial infection. Wine yeast is one of the few organisms capable of existing in an acidic environment (acetic acid-forming bacteria being the other common example). The presence of acid not only protects the wine itself from spoilage but ensures that food poisoning bacteria, which cannot live in high acid concentrations, are unlikely to be present.

A range of fruit acids are involved in winemaking, - tartaric, malic and citric being the main ones. These different acids present us with a problem when deciding the degree of acidity as all acids vary in strength. The reason for this is the acids owe their activity to their ability to let go of one of the hydrogen particles which they contain. Some release these far more readily than others, making them stronger acids. Since the fruit juices used to make the wine contain more than one type of acid this complicates the process of establishing the total amount of active acid present, and any amounts which might have to be added. To avoid confusion, and to allow for accurate comparisons between fruits irrespective of which acids they actually contain, it is usual to quote acid strengths relative to sulphuric acid. Of course, no wine must will actually contain sulphuric acid, it is employed simply as an arbitrary standard - used solely for comparison purposes. It is usual to quote the quantity of acid present in parts per thousand (ppt). Each ppt is one tenth of one percent.

Types of Acid
a) Tartaric acid, this is the main acid of grape juice, but it is not that common in other country winemaking ingredients. Often thought to impart vinosity to a drink many winemakers like to include fifty percent tartaric acid in any acid additions to the must. Excess tartaric acid may be precipitated out as long needle shaped crystals as the

wine matures.

b) Malic acid takes its name from apples *(Malus)* - it is the main acid of this fruit. It is the most important acid of gooseberries and rhubarb as well as most members of the *Prunus* family - plums, damsons, cherries, apricots, and peaches, although the latter two also contain important amounts of citric acid. Malic acid is present in large amounts in grape juice, in some cases contributing up to a third of the total acidity.

c) Citric acid, present as the main acid in *Citrus* and many other fruits used in home winemaking. Its inclusion is considered desirable in all recipes to ensure a smooth fermentation, but it is not always necessary to add it as it will already be present in many fruit. Citric acid may be used as the sole acid for adding to a must or a wine after fermentation is complete. It has the disadvantage that when present in large quantities the wine can acquire a typical citrus fruit taste.

Acid levels

The acid levels in the majority of commercial table wines vary between 5.0-7.0 ppt although some of the harsher cheaper varieties almost certainly have higher values. Full bodied sweet dessert wines often have acid levels of 6.0-8.0 ppt possibly as high as 10.0 ppt, although ports may be far lower than this and sherries can be as low as 3.0 ppt. Several of the more successful fruit show wines tend to have values of about 8.0-9.0 ppt acid. A little extra acid certainly makes a wine stand out amongst a crowd, but take care that you do not overdo it! It should be realised that a high sugar level will act as a buffer, dulling the senses and minimising the sensation of acidity, higher alcohol levels tend to act in a similar manner. In the presence of large excesses of sugar acid may still be present. It has not been neutralised or destroyed, but simply our taste buds are overwhelmed by the sugar and can no longer detect the acid.

Exact measurements of acidity are a useful guide, but the combined effect of the other components will modify the sensation and it cannot be stressed too strongly that taste must be the final arbiter on what does or does not constitute a balanced wine. Scientific aids are useful, but they are no substitute for a well trained palate.

The quantity of acid that they contain is one of the factors which will govern the maximum quantity of most fruits which you may include in a gallon of must - although other items such as flavour and tannin levels may be the determining factor in some cases. With blackberries the amount of acid governs the quantity that can be employed whereas with the very low acid elderberries it is the strong flavour which is the restricting influence.

The following table shows the total quantity of acid that 3lb of fruit will provide to a gallon of must. It is assumed that the liquid has been efficiently extracted by pressing or other suitable means.

Fruit	Total acid ppt (3lb/gallon of must)
Apples	0.8-3.0
Bananas	2.0-2.5
Blackberries	3.0-3.5
Blackcurrants	7.0-7.5
Cherries (dessert)	1.5-3.0
Cherries (Morello)	5.0-6.0
Damsons	7.0-8.0

Elderberries	1.5-2.0
Gooseberries	2.0-6.0
Loganberries	4.5-5.0
Oranges	3.0
Oranges(Seville)	5.0-6.0
Peaches	2.0-2.5
Pears	1.0-2.0
Plums	4.0-5.0
Pineapples	3.0
Raspberries	4.0-5.0
Redcurrant	4.0
Rhubarb	5.5-7.0
Strawberries	3.0

A can of grape juice concentrate will, when diluted, contribute between 4.0-6.0 ppt to a gallon of wine. Both raisins and sultanas will add very small amounts of acid to a must and these can usually be ignored in any calculations.

The foregoing is only an approximation. The exact value will depend upon the variety, the time of harvesting and the efficiency of extraction but the figures may be used with confidence to compound a must. Any additions can be made to the finished wine. Using these figures it is unlikely that you will get a wine which is too high in acid, but should this occur, you can solve the problem by blending.

Accurate determination of acidity in a wine must
Alkalis are substances chemically opposite in their action to acids and cancel them out. Use can be made of this principle to establish accurately how much acid is present in a wine must. Given this information, additional amounts

of acid may be added or the liquid diluted with alkalis.

Certain chemical substances - term indicators - change their colour in alkaline solution compared with that in acid media. The indicator usually used to determining acid levels in wines is phenolphthalein, which is colourless in acid solution and a purple red colour, reminiscent of freshly pressed elderberry juice, in an alkaline solution. The colour change is easily detected in white wines. With reds it is a little more difficult, but with a little practise you will soon become proficient in the technique. At the neutral point you can detect a darkening of the red colour which some people find easier to see when the liquid is held up to an artificial light. But decide for yourself what best suits your eyesight.

The method of determining the acidity consists of placing a measured amount of wine must or fruit juice in a container and adding a few drops of an indicator. Dropwise additions of the alkali sodium hydroxide (caustic soda) are made until the indicator changes colour. The change is sudden rather than gradual, at the neutral point one drop of alkali is sufficient to bring about a dramatic effect which you cannot miss as the liquid changes from colourless to red. The amount of sodium hydroxide added is directly related to the acidity of the liquid. Since the alkali can be made up to any desired strength acid testing kits may be produced where the acidity concentration in ppt is equivalent to the volume of alkali added.

pH Scale
We have already established that acids owe their sharp taste to their ability to release bonded hydrogen units and that this differs in the various types of acid. A method has

been found of actually measuring the number of freed hydrogen particles and this provides a direct way of establishing the acidity of any solution. The particles of hydrogen which the acid releases, termed ions, are electrically charged and any solution containing acids will have a potential for a current to flow due to their presence - a potential of Hydrogen. This has lead to the pH scale which measures directly the number of hydrogen ions present in the solution. Cheap methods using chemical indicators tend to give variable results in all but the most skilled hands. The more accurate method of determining the pH of any solution is to measure the voltage generated between two standard electrodes. This requires relatively expensive equipment and is an unnecessary complication. The home winemaker is advised to use only titration to determine acidities. In spite of this, many books still tend to discuss wines in terms of pH, and should you wish to progress your studies further, it will be necessary to understand the subject even though its practical application may be limited.

Water contains hydrogen and one in every ten million molecules of water breaks down naturally to release the hydrogen ion. The neutral substance water is given the pH value of 7. In beer one in every ten thousand molecules break down to release the hydrogen ion and this is given the pH value of 4. It will be seen that the more acidic a solution is the lower will be its pH.

The PH scale for the substances related to winemaking are:

Vinegar	2.0
Lemon Juice	2.0
Sherry	3.5

Sparkling Wine	3.0
Table Wine	3.0-3.5
Beer	4.0
Distilled water	7.0
Drinking water	7.5

Body

The body of the wine is the weight which it has in the mouth; it is the thickness of the liquid. Body is due to the presence of dissolved solids. These solids include non-fermentable sugars, various non-sugar solids, and glycerine, which is not a solid at all but a thick viscous liquid soluble in both water and alcohol. Glycerine occurs naturally in Sauternes after the noble rot, being a byproduct of the Botrytis metabolism. Some fruits are rich in non-fermentable dissolved solids, and are ideal for inclusion in a range of musts, providing that they do not possess a strong flavour which will detract from that of the other ingredients. In traditional winemaking a range of materials, including pea and bean pods, wheat, barley, and even malt, were used to provide body. Today we rely on more conventional materials, raisins and sultanas, grape juice concentrate and bananas.

In dessert wines the fermentable, but unconverted, sugar makes the largest contribution to the body of the liquid. Artificial sweeteners do not have this structural effect, and whilst they may be acceptable in terms of taste (except for the lightest of sweet table wines), are easily distinguished from the better naturally sweet products.

As well as providing weight, these unfermented solids have another very important role - to perform as a buffer between the taste buds and the sharp astringent components of the liquid. Overcoming this buffering effect is one of the reasons why a full-bodied dessert wine requires half as much again acid as a light table wine.

Flavour, Bouquet and Aroma
These are the most complex aspects of a wine - impossible even to attempt to analyse in any scientific manner. Completely subjective, their assessment is the real skill of winemanship. It is the skill in assessing these factors above all else that leads to a real understanding of wine and how to make it. Factors such as alcohol, sugar, and acids, will all contribute but the most influential group of compounds are the esters. Esters are formed as a result of acids combining with alcohols. In wine there are two types; those naturally present in the fruits from which the wine was made, and others which form as a result of fermentation. In the wine's early life it is the former which often predominates. But esters will break down to release the acids and alcohols from which they were originally made. With aging, the wine loses the taste of the fruit and takes on a character all of its own as a result of the formation of new flavourings. But this is an over-simplification as other processes occur with time; oxidation, as a result of the minute quantities of air which are always associated with wine however careful you are, and substances such as oak tannins which may be dissolved out of the wood, and the presence of flavourings other than esters in the original ingredients.

Balance
The balance of a wine is the inter-relationship between all of its component parts - alcohol, acid, sugar, tannin and

flavour. For a wine to be balanced, all these factors must complement each other without one being allowed to dominate. This will only occur if they are present in similar relative amounts.

A table wine is balanced, because all the main features are at low levels, resulting in light flavour low acidity drinks. Dessert wines are balanced because everything is present in relatively large amounts. In other styles such as social wines all are present in intermediate amounts.

Although there are some aspects of wine which we can clearly measure, such as the alcoholic strength, the majority of the most important features are sensations on the palate. We will never be able to measure or define all of them exactly, and will always have to rely on that most critical of detecting devices - our own sense of taste. For this reason it will never be possible to mix ingredients in a factory to produce an artificial wine. It is us who will always need to ferment it. It is an art and a science but the more knowledge we have of the process the better we are equipped to perform the task.

2: UNDERSTANDING WINEMAKING

Many homemade wines are not as good as they could or should be. Expensive ingredients are wasted because the vintner attempts to turn them into wine by using unsound methods which are doomed to failure from the start. Understanding winemaking is an essential ingredient of success - without appreciating the processes involved you are relying on luck, totally dependant upon recipes and not qualified to make adjustments and correct mistakes.

Confronted with complex scientific formulae, incomprehensible language and unclear explanations it is easy to understand why would-be winemakers tend to ignore this most important part of their wine education. But winemaking is a natural phenomenon. It is simple and anyone can understand it and go on to harness man's first technological discovery to their advantage. The theory of winemaking should be viewed not as a step back into the classroom, but the key which unlocks the secret of success.

The transformation of a liquid into a wine is complex and involves several chemical changes occurring simultaneously. Reactions which will produce the perfect drink occur naturally but unfortunately so do other changes which result in a sour, evil smelling, undrinkable liquid.

The art of winemaking is to create conditions under which the desired changes occur and the wine spoiling reactions do not.

SUGAR, ALCOHOL AND FERMENTATION

Winemaking is only possible through the existence of a simple single celled fungus - yeast. Examined under the microscope this plant is seen to consist of individual oval shaped cells, often attached to their neighbours in groups of three or four. Some cells are seen to have small buds - these are the new plants developing.

All living things need a food supply to produce the energy to sustain life and, in the case of yeast, it is sugar. How the yeast does this and the way in which it changes the sugar will depend upon whether or not air is present.

Where there is plenty of air dissolved in the water the yeast will use the abundance of oxygen to break down the sugar and release carbon dioxide and water together with a large amount of energy.

Sugar + Oxygen — > Carbon Dioxide + Water + High Energy

This life process, which is totally dependant on the presence of air, is referred to as aerobic.

When the oxygen initially dissolved in the water has been used up it will not be replenished due to the insulating action of the layer of carbon dioxide which has formed above the liquid.

Unlike most other living organisms, once its air supply has been exhausted yeast automatically switches over to a backup metabolic system which is not dependant on the presence of oxygen. It is this alternative life style of the yeast that produces the wine. The yeast now releases the energy trapped in the sugar by a mechanism that is far less efficient, but which produces the byproduct alcohol in the process.

Sugar —> Carbon Dioxide + Alcohol + Low Energy

Life processes without air are referred to as anaerobic.

Being less efficient this is never the yeast's preferred route, and if air is again allowed to dissolve in the liquid as will happen during racking, the yeast will temporarily revert to its former alcohol free lifestyle.

To make quality wines it is essential that we stop air from dissolving in an established must, thereby forcing the yeast to liberate alcohol to obtain its energy.

Types of Sugar
There are many different types of sugar. It is the simplest sugars, glucose and fructose, found in grape juice, concentrates and a variety of fruits, that yeast converts into alcohol. The winemaker provides much, often most, of the sugar as sucrose which consists of a unit of each of glucose and fructose joined together. Converting sucrose into alcohol involves the yeast in an extra operation - known as 'inversion' - the breaking down of the double sugar into its two component parts.

This presents no problem to the yeast which possesses an additional enzyme which automatically converts the sucrose into the prefered forms.

Sucrose + Water ——> Glucose + Fructose (in the presence of yeast)

Alcohol is a waste product which will poison the environment and ultimately kills its creator, the yeast, thus setting a limit to the amount of alcohol that can be obtained by fermentation.

A good wine yeast will produce about sixteen percent alcohol although higher levels are obtainable. To achieve these, you will require a special strain of yeast and it will be necessary to maintain a temperature of about 22C (72F) and a smooth uninterrupted fermentation (except for the feeding process at the conclusion).

Very high levels of alcohol are seldom necessary except as a base for making liqueurs.

Under ideal conditions sixteen percent alcohol can be obtained from about 2¾ pounds of sugar per gallon (275gm/litre). But varying amounts of sugar will be burnt up yielding greatly reduced quantities of alcohol. This non productive loss of sugar occurs mainly during the growth stage of the fermentation process and the actual quantities that are used before the yeast becomes inactive can be in excess of 3 pounds per gallon (300gm/litre). This will not adversely affect the quality of the wines. Any sugar remaining after fermentation will bestow a sweet taste to the wine.

The quantity of sugar which you need to add to a wine must to provide a particular level alcohol can be found by using a hydrometer (see page 73). Alcohol levels calculated from gravity readings tend to be approximate unless you are very careful at all stages of fermentation.

Feeding

Water is drawn through the cell wall being attracted by
the salts that are contained in the body of the yeast. But if
the sugar outside the cell wall is more concentrated than
the dissolved solids within, it will drain the water out of
the yeast, dehydrate and kill it. To avoid any problems
sugar should always be dissolved before being added to a
must. When making high alcohol wines it is not advisable
to provide all the sugar at the start of fermentation as you
are more likely to be left with more sugar than the balance can carry. Opinions differ as to whether the stress
produced as a result of the stop-start approach actually
inhibits the yeast from producing the final traces of alcohol.

THE REQUIREMENTS OF YEAST

Like all living organisms, yeast requires the correct environment if it is to prosper.

Temperature

Yeast only ferments a wine must over a limited temperature range. Whilst the exact values will depend upon the
particular strain, below about 7C (45F) most yeasts becomes dormant, above about 35C (95F) they are rendered
inactive and ultimately die. The higher the temperature
within this range the faster that the fermentation is completed. Unfortunately if the temperature is too high the
yeast itself can produce off flavours and the wine will
become cooked. Slow fermentation tends to produce far
better wines, but values which are too low can result in
stuck ferments, as can also be the case at very high tem-

peratures. The optimum temperature range for top quality wines is 15-22C (59-72F). Seek to maintain this value throughout fermentation.

Acidity

We have already discussed the role of acid in the balance of a wine. It has a second important role in the fermentation process itself. To grow correctly, yeast requires an acid solution, without it the wine acquires a medicinal taste. Fortunately the level of acidity which favours the yeast's development is the same level which gives the wine the correct degree of 'bite'.

Many fruits contain acids which may supply some or all of that which is required. Other ingredients contain no acid and the necessary amount must be provided by the winemaker. Good published recipes will include reasonable estimates of the amount of acid required. But it may be inaccurate for a number of reasons. Variety of fruit, the stage at which it was gathered, and seasonal variations as a result of the weather, all have an influence on the actual amount of acid naturally present. With all of the recipes given in this book you may make them in the confidence that they will not develop off flavours during fermentation. If on tasting you feel that the acidity requires adjusting you can correct it by means of blending after fermentation is complete.

Remember the palate is the most sensitive indicator of all factors affecting taste, the final arbiter superior to any scientific test.

Blending is for minor adjustments. To avoid acid levels far removed from the ideal you should determine the amount of acid present and make any necessary adjustment when compounding your own recipes.

Nutrients
As well as sugar, which it uses to provide energy and part
of its body structure, yeast requires other nutrients: nitro-
gen as nitrates for the protein of its body tissue; phos-
phates to create the enzymes which are the catalysts that
make all of the life processes possible, and thiamin (vita-
min B1) which aids the release of the energy stored in the
sugar. It is realised now that yeast, like all living things,
requires a whole range of nutritional vitamins and minerals. These materials are only required in minute amounts,
and there is sufficient naturally present in grape juice, but
they may be missing from many of the other ingredients
used in winemaking. To avoid problems and, as a further
precaution against stuck ferments, it is advisable to add a
combined yeast nutrient - many forms of which may have
very complex formulations - at the beginning of fermentation. Do not exceed the recommended dose as any un-
used nutrients will bestow a salty taste on the drink and
lead to an over-vigorous fermentation.

THE RISE AND FALL OF THE YEAST'S ACTIVITY
Yeast during its life in a wine must goes through four
distinct phases.

The Lag Phase
The winemaking process is initiated by adding a yeast
starter to the liquid, held in a container large enough to
provide an adequate air space above.

No activity is noticed for several hours. During this time the yeast is adjusting to its new environment and growing, yet still only producing very minute quantities of carbon dioxide. The small amount of gas is dissolving in the water and giving no noticeable sign of activity.

Rapid Growth (logarithmic) Phase
The first visible sign that the process has started is the appearance of a few small bubbles on the surface of the liquid. This will be noticed after one or two days depending upon yeast type, nature of the must and, more importantly, the temperature. The slight effervescence rapidly increases to a vigorous froth. At this stage the yeast cells, confronted with an abundance of food, dissolved oxygen and plenty of room to grow, are breeding rapidly. In order that this can happen the must is exposed to the air so that the yeast can extract the maximum amount of energy from the sugar. Reproduction is a process which requires the expending of a great deal of energy and you must not attempt to inhibit the access of air at this stage.

The large volumes of carbon dioxide that are being liberated will saturate the must, in the process making the liquid buoyant and causing any solids to rise to the surface. The presence of this large quantity of gas will stop the oxygen of the air dissolving in the liquid and will itself slow down this particular stage. Stirring the liquid daily aids the fermentation by helping to release the carbon dioxide and allowing more air to enter the liquid.

Like all steps in the fermentation process the time taken for this particular stage will depend upon the variables. Time scales given in recipes should only be used as a guide. They will vary even between batches made at the same time in the same house. Always keep a daily watch on the must. Note when the vigorous head reaches its peak and when it subsides to a gentle bubbling - the sign that the growth phase has finished.

The cessation of the rapid growth stage signals the arrival of the maximum number of yeast cells that the volume of liquid can sustain and which the food supply can support. The only additional cells that the environment will be able to support will be to replace those which have died.

The finish of the growth phase heralds the end of the need to supply the yeast with oxygen. This gas, which was previously essential to start off the fermentation process, will from now on destroy the wine in various ways and the liquid must be continuously protected from it. It is at this stage that we transfer the liquid from the fermentation bucket to the demijohn.

Stationary Phase

The yeast now begins making alcohol in earnest and the only sign of activity is the steady emergence of carbon dioxide from the bubbler.

Gradually this bubbling begins to decrease. During the stationary state sugar is being progressively used up whilst at the same time alcohol is being formed. A declining food source, and the emergence of a progressively hostile environment as the toxic waste product alcohol builds up, means that the yeast has got to increasingly fight to stay alive. A battle that it is ultimately destined to lose.

Decline Phase

As time progresses, the rate of conversion of sugar decreases until it reaches a critical point where the concentration of alcohol is such that it poisons all the remaining yeast cells. At this stage the fermentation is complete.

This sequence of events, during which the maximum tolerable alcohol level is reached, will only take place if conditions are correct. Under certain circumstances fermentation can prematurely cease, and will only recommence if the right conditions return.

The two most common reasons for this are:

1. Activity has stopped as a result of the temperature being allowed to drop below the level at which yeast is active. When the atmosphere becomes warmer fermentation starts up again. It is this reactivity which causes corks to pop in the early summer.

2. In dry wine production insufficient sugar is provided to produce the maximum tolerable alcohol level. Even in totally clear wine there will be dormant yeast cells which may cause the recommencement of fermentation if additional sweetening sugar is added.

There is no guarantee that a wine which has previously stopped working - called a stuck ferment - will readily start again. The further that the stationary phase has progressed the more hostile will be the environment towards the yeast and the greater the barrier that it will have to overcome to start work again. Often it is only after a great deal of effort that it is possible to recommence fermentation. Every care should be taken to ensure that ideal and consistent conditions are provided and maintained throughout all stages in order that fermentation does not cease prematurely. Only in this way will you obtain high alcohol levels.

In sparkling wine production, where fermentation is deliberately allowed to cease and is then restarted, the technique is only successful with low alcohol wines.

The four phase description suggests that all yeast cells are behaving identically at any particular time. In practice the sequence of events is slightly more complicated. Fermentation is never totally aerobic, very early on during the growth phase the liquid at the bottom of the bucket will become devoid of oxygen and small amounts of alcohol will be produced. The opposite occurs after racking when small quantities of oxygen will have dissolved in the must and (unless it is sulphited) some aerobic activity will take place. Generally these slight variations may be ignored although one important consequence of the early formation of the alcohol is dependent upon its ability to dissolve materials out of fruit which are unaffected by water. As a result, as soon as any alcohol is liberated the composition of the must will change. Initially the effect is beneficial, esters, which make up the bouquet of flowers, readily dissolve in the alcohol as do other flavour-producing essential oils. But the longer that the newly formed alcohol remains in contact with any solid material the greater the range of chemicals that it will leach out and the harsher the wine becomes. This is another important reason why the liquid should not be allowed to remain on the must after the growth phase.

Oxygen and Carbon Dioxide

We have seen that acid and alkalis are opposites and tend to neutralise each other. The other two opposites involved in winemaking are oxygen, usually present as air, and carbon dioxide.

Oxygen supports life, the majority of microbes which

infect a wine can not survive in the absence of air and are totally dependant upon the gas. Chemically, oxygen is very active. It adds to a large range of materials to produce new substances with different tastes and colours. The addition of oxygen to a wine is termed oxidation and the wine is said to be oxidised. Wines which have been oxidised will have a completely different character from those which have not. Usually this taste is unacceptable in all drinks except sherry types, and in smaller amounts in dessert wines; another reason why we need to exclude air from the wine at all stages after the growth phase.

During the long maturation period small quantities of air will gradually come into contact with the wine. These minute amounts of oxygen are actually beneficial at this stage, bringing about subtle changes which enhance the development of the flavour.

Carbon dioxide is chemically inactive and does not support life. It is heavier than air and throughout the growth phase, when a large amount of the gas is generated, it creates a blanket over the surface of the fermenting liquids, protecting it from infection. Any germs which enter the liquid will be smothered by the carbon dioxide, and air will be unable to reach the liquid.

THE RELATIONSHIP BETWEEN YEAST AND SULPHUR DIOXIDE

It is as if nature specifically designed yeast to make wine. In addition to its ability to form alcohol it has four distinct advantages over the wine destroying organisms which compete to live in the must.

1. Yeasts can survive higher levels of alcohol than most

microbes, which are destroyed in a 12+ percent alcohol solution. Since wines with higher alcohol levels are far less likely to become infected and develop off flavours 12 percent alcohol should be seen as the lower level for quality homemade wines. This will allow you to make the fullest range including the very best table wines. If such levels are too high, you may dilute at the time of serving with lemonade or other mixers.

2. Yeasts can survive and produce alcohol in the presence of a solution saturated with carbon dioxide. Such conditions are intolerable to the majority of spoilage organisms which are totally aerobic.

3. Yeasts live and grow in a relatively high acidity. Food poisoning bacteria cannot survive in these conditions, which means that problems will not occur as a result of prolonged storage of wines. Vinegaring bacteria can survive high acid levels but they require oxygen and need not be a problem.

4. Yeasts can tolerate levels of sulphur dioxide which will control the majority of spoilage organisms. Winemaking yeast also has a higher tolerance to sulphur dioxide than wild yeasts, which are suppressed by the concentration used in winemaking. This increased resistance to sulphur dioxide used at the correct concentration allows you to control all organisms harmful to winemaking, whilst letting the yeast survive and develop without any competition for the available food and space.

For top quality winemaking sulphur dioxide must be used. Whilst boiling water is at least as effective at killing spoilage organisms it can slightly char the natural sugars present producing caramelisation which in the majority of cases is undesirable.

Grapes, apples, and even potatoes, darken when cut and exposed. Sulphur dioxide neutralises the browning effects of air and will allow a wine to retain its colour. Such protection is not afforded using the boiling water method.

When a wine has finished fermenting, sulphur dioxide will protect the liquids from spoilage organisms and retard the wine yeast from regaining its activity. With the delicate light table wines which reveal the slightest imperfection it is necessary to maintain the correct levels of sulphur dioxide throughout. Heavier dessert wines with their higher strength, astringency and sugar, are far more robust, and the use of sulphur dioxide after fermentation is complete is not so critical.

Sulphur dioxide's presence is detected by a strong drying taste at the back of the throat and care should be taken to ensure that excessive amounts are not used.

HARMFUL PROCESSES
Autolysis
Throughout the stationary and decline phases yeast cells are dying and falling to the bottom of the container together with minute pieces of vegetable matter previously suspended in the liquid. Gradually a layer of dead material settles at the bottom of the demijohn. Although the particles are dead, enzymes of decay suppressed when the materials were alive become active and begin to breakdown the cells. Strong, musty off flavours reminiscent of damp and decay quickly develop. Unless this solid material is separated from the wine the enzymes of decay will render it undrinkable!

Malolactic Fermentation

An additional fermentation brought about by bacteria can occur in an otherwise finished wine. This results in the harsh malic acid present in many fruits, including grapes, being changed into the softer more mellow lactic acid. Referred to as malolactic fermentation the condition is sometimes sought in commercial wine production. In amateur winemaking it is usually the result of carelessness, its arrival an accident, and the value of any improvements questionable.

Many poorly made wines, where adequate care was not taken to maintain the correct temperature, referment in the Spring. This is simply the result of the rise in temperature and not, as is often incorrectly stated, malolactic fermentation.

Malolactic fermentation can be brought about by different bacteria, the commonest of which is lactobacillus which is responsible for souring milk. The bacteria is everywhere, as is illustrated by the ease with which milk sours, and will readily find its way into wine. For the microbe to be active in a wine it requires oxygen which can enter during the racking. Sulphiting the liquid at this stage will control the bacteria. Malolactic fermentation will only occur if sulphur dioxide is omitted and a temperature of at least 18C (15F) is maintained. Whilst the process can result in mellower wines, the conditions needed for it to occur will favour the growth of spoilage organisms and it should not be encouraged.

3: THE BASIC INGREDIENTS

We have established the main components of a wine and have seen how by fermentation juices may be changed into an alcoholic drink. But the quality and character of the wine will be controlled directly by the ingredients which go into its manufacture. However carefully a wine is made, however long it is matured, you will never make a good drink unless the right ingredients were used in the correct amounts in the first place.

The home winemaker is always attempting to reach his goal by compounding a must which the yeast and the laws of chemistry will convert to the drink of his desire. Good wines do not occur by accident - they are the result of carefully planned recipes. The winemaker is the creator of every brew - the artist blending his paints.

There are basically two types of wine:

Single Fruit Wines
Today such wines are seldom made, but rhubarb is one of the few remaining true examples of a single fruit wine made from just one ingredient with added sugar. Far more common is that group of wines made from one fruit together with dried grapes, raisins, or sultanas and these

are also referred to as single fruit wines. However, in reality they are either simply fruit flavoured raisin wines or blended wines.

Blended Must Wines

This group contains the vast majority of homemade wines with the blending of the ingredients taking place in the fermentation bucket. As soon as you provide a second fruit your wine is in fact a blend. In principle there is no difference between a wine which is blended before or after fermentation, but whilst many wine makers feel happy creating a blended must there still remains some reluctance to blend finished wines. When considering blended wines it is necessary to understand what is meant by the main ingredient. This is the ingredient whose character comes through in the finished wine. It is not necessarily the ingredient which is present in the largest amount. When making an elderflower wine, only a few grams of petals are added to the must, but nevertheless it is the dominant factor, whose bouquet and flavour dominate.

INGREDIENTS

Grapes

Grapes remain the most important ingredient in country winemaking, they may be used either as the dried fruits, raisins and sultanas, as grape juice concentrate, or increasingly pure grape juice.

Grape Juice Concentrate

This is such an important ingredient in modern winemaking that it is worth knowing exactly what it is and how it is prepared.

There are variations on the method of preparation but the general procedure remains the same. White grape juice concentrates are made by stemming the grapes, crushing and the free run juice collected. Pectic enzyme is then added to stop the concentrate from forming jelly later in the operation and sulphur dioxide is provided to prevent oxidative browning. To make red concentrates, the grapes are crushed and heated to between 60C (140F) and 70C (145F) bringing about the extraction of the red pigment from the skin. The free run juice is collected and the residues pressed. The two types of juice are mixed, pectic enzyme added and the whole allowed to stand.

Evaporating the water from the juice at atmospheric pressure requires a temperature which would caramelise the sugars. The problem is overcome by placing the liquid in vacuum pans which continually draws the steam off of the juice causing it to boil at a much lower temperature. The greater the vacuum the lower the temperature at which the liquid boils. The juice is usually heated to about 45C (110F). Even at this low temperature, much of the delicate aroma of the grape juice is lost, being evaporated off in the steam. This steam is then passed through a condenser or liquefier. The part which liquefies at the lowest temperature will contain those esters and other substances responsible for the most delicate aspects of the flavour. This fraction is then returned to the concentrate.

Clearly such products contain all of the most important vinifying ingredients of the grape and may be used, either for making a wine with the addition of only water and sugar, or used in smaller quantities as an additive. Red wines made solely from concentrates will differ from their counterparts prepared directly from the grape in that there is no fermentation conducted in the presence of the fruit. This leads to a reduction in the level of alcohol soluble components, with lower tannin levels giving a noticeably softer wine, verging on bland with some of the cheaper concentrate wines. The good winemaker will recognise this and adjust the must accordingly. Virtually all concentrates require the addition of sugar. This can be due to two reasons - there may not have been a full gallon of juice concentrated to produce the contents of the can or, alternatively, if there were, there may still be insufficient natural sugar in the grapes. Even grapes used in commercial wine production do not always contain enough sugar and sometimes it is necessary to add extra usually as grape sugars, a process termed chapitalisation. Grape juice concentrate is a high density sugar solution and should always be stored in cool conditions as the sugars will caramelise very easily.

Not all grape juice concentrates are the same. Like commercial wines they vary with the type of grape used, the area in which they were grown, as well as the degree of concentration and the method of removing the water. Whilst the winemaker need not be too concerned with the technical aspects, he should appreciate that these differences exist and should compare the various products on the market. With grape juice concentrates price is usually a good guide to quality.

Pure or unconcentrated grape juice
Grape juice is prepared by crushing and gathering the juice from stemmed grapes. The white is lightly sulphited to protect the colour, red juice is slightly heated to extract the pigment. The juices are then filtered, pasteurised to

stop fermentation by natural yeasts and sold in cartons. Grape juice has two roles in home winemaking - either as a simple additive or for topping up after racking. It is always preferable to water for this process as it does not dilute the liquid, and being added late, increases the grapiness of the wine and helps to develop the vinosity. Generally the use of this ingredient is limited to a fifth of the total volume of the liquid. The difference between various brands tends to have less influence on the finished product than when using grape juice concentrate.

Raisins and Sultanas
These represent the oldest method of adding grapes to a home made wine, and due to the arrival of grape juices have become less popular in recent years. This is unfortunate as they remain excellent ingredients of the highest quality with a direct parallel in the commercial world. In a limited number of wines raisins are added to the must, in others the grapes are allowed to remain on the vines until raisining has taken place and the grapes which now have a high sugar, low moisture, content used. However the practice is not widespread.

Raisins are made from red grapes, sultanas from white - both are produced by drying the fruit, a process which can liberate pectin. Consequently whenever these fruits are employed you should include pectic enzyme in the must prior to adding the yeast. Raisins are generally only suitable for including in red wines and are especially good with dessert wines. Lighter types can be used for tawny and sherry type wines. Whilst sultanas can be used in all wines, they do not make the contribution to the complex character of a red dessert wine which you would expect from a raisin. When making light wines, whites, rosés and the lightest of reds choose a white to golden sultana.

There are several different types of raisins and sultanas and the following varieties each bestow their own individual character on the wine.

Raisins

Muscatel, the most scented and well developed flavour of all raisins, can be obtained either stoned or unstoned.

Australian raisins excellent for winemaking.

Chilean Raisins produce a well developed vinosity in the wine.

Afghan black raisins, sharp tangy fruit particularly suited for making full bodied desserts.

Sultanas

Light golden sultanas are suited to virtually every type of white wine.

Those slightly brown in colour, the result of oxidation and caramelisation, are best suited to sherry and dessert type wines rather than flower or light table wines.

To improve the appearance and the ease of separation of individual fruits some raisins and sultanas are covered with a thin layer of vegetable oil. Although this will tend to float to the surface of the water it is better to avoid the problem by not using fruits prepared in this way. As winemaking is not the major use of raisins and sultanas to ensure that you are getting the fruit best suited to your purpose always go to a specialist homebrew or health food shop. Try to familiarise yourself with the taste of as many different varieties of dried fruit as possible as their role in winemaking is so important.

FRESH FRUIT

Harvesting of Fruit

The professional vigneron will carefully watch the crop ripening and on the precise day that he considers the grapes to be at the optimum state for winemaking harvest them. Only if we pay the same attention to detail can we hope to get similar results, but all too often this is an aspect of winemaking which is overlooked.

The development and ripening of fruit is another complex natural process. During the early stages in its development the fruit is unappetising, high in acid and starch, low in sugars. As the seeds reach maturity the flesh surrounding them changes, with the acids and starches replaced with sugars and flavourings. The fruit reach a level of perfection and it is now that they should be harvested. After this stage they soon begin to decay. Enzymes of destruction start to dominate, breaking down the fruit which begins to take on an earthy taste. This decay, similar to the autolysis of the lees, produces a musty taste in the wine. If such fruit is used then the wine commences life with a musty taste, and it does not matter how careful you are in the making, it will always posses an off flavour. Ruthlessly discard any overripe, bruised or damaged fruits. Overripe fruits may also be suffering from the starts of fungal infections which will lead to musty flavours in a similar way. Pay very careful attention to fruit selection, it can be the most important factor in winemaking.

Note: Quantities given should only be used as a guide, they do not necessarily correspond to the specially compounded recipes given later in the book.

RED WINEMAKING INGREDIENTS

Blackberries

One of the most important of all winemaking ingredients suitable as a base for all red wines providing colour, flavour, and acid. Blackberries can be used to the extent of four pounds per gallon in table wines, rising to six pounds per gallon for full port type desserts. There is an extended season from early August until late September. Although apparently ripe, the early fruits tend to be high in acid with the late season fruits almost bland. Those gathered during the last week in August or first week in September make the best wine - but this date will differ to some extent depending upon the locality. For growing in the garden choose the variety Oregon Thornless which carries a heavy crop of monster berries that are slightly less acidic than most wild varieties. As a generalisation, wild fruits tend to have more pronounced flavour than the cultivated forms, possibly the result of gathering from the many hybrids which make up a hedgerow. Blackberry wines commence life deep red in colour. With age this changes to a warm golden brown and when older still is a rich gold tinged with red. Where blackberry is the major ingredient the wine definitely improves with correct keeping for up to five years possibly longer. It may also be drunk in its first year when it is a very fruity wine.

Elderberries

A very useful ingredient but not as versatile as blackberries, the very high tannin content restricting the amount of fruit which may be included in a must. Elderberries always produce far better wines when they are included as part of a blended must, particularly with blackberries.

They provide little acid or body but help to develop a full red wine flavour. Elderberries should never be fermented on the must for more than three days, otherwise excessive amounts of tannin will be extracted and it will take several years for the wine to become sufficiently mellow to drink. It is far better to extract the juice by separating it from the skin, which will give a wine that is drinkable within three months. Such wines do lack some of the character of the elderberry, and this can be provided by including a cupful of the berries in the bucket and allowing fermentation to proceed in their presence. When a glass of young elderberry wine is held up to the light the ring at the top of the liquid has a deep well developed purple tinge. Within about a year this hue will have disappeared but the deep red colour of the wine will remain for several years.

If practical, allow the fruit to remain on the bushes until just before the berries begin to shrivel. Within reason, and providing that decay has not set in, the older the fruit the better the wine. There would appear to be several wild hybrids of elders, certain differences such as the shapes of the berries are discernable on careful observation. With experience you will discover that the finesse of a wine can depend upon the bushes from which the fruit was collected. Where a bush has provided good fruit in the past try to use it again in the future.

There is a colourless sort, the so-called golden elderberry. This does not make a good wine.

Damsons
An excellent ingredient. It is high in both acid and tannin with a very rich flavour, and is ideal for providing depth

of character to a red wine. It is suitable for lifting elderberry wines and for producing complex flavours in desserts. Use a pound per gallon in table wines rising to two
in desserts. Damsons have the disadvantage that they contain a relatively large stone for the quantity of flesh. They
are used by cutting each fruit to aid the extraction of materials but it is impractical to attempt to remove the seeds
before making the wine.

Sloes
A greatly over-estimated ingredient, unless you can allow them to remain on the bushes until the end of October. They tend to be very high in acid and tannin and
little else. Colour is late developing and wines made from
early gathered fruit tend to be rosé in colour. Quantities
as for damsons.

Loganberries
Another top class ingredient. They are high in acid and
tannin which tends to bring the best out of the other fruits
without tending to dominate the wine. Wait until the loganberries have acquire a deep purple coloration before
attempting to harvest them. Use with other fruit at the
rate of a pound per gallon for table wines and two pounds
for desserts. Lightly crush the fruit before placing in the
bucket, fermentation may proceed in their presence for a
week. Loganberries appear to make better wines than the
other widely grown raspberry/blackberry cross, the
tayberry.

Blackcurrants
An ingredient to be used in limited amounts as it has such

a pronounced flavour. A half to a pound per gallon is the maximum of the high acid fruit which should be used. Lightly crush and add to the fermentation bucket where they can remain for a week.

Bilberries
A useful if somewhat rare ingredient. With medium acid and tannin they can be used as the sole ingredient at the rate of three pounds for a table wine or five pounds for a dessert. Where lesser quantities are available these may be included in place of another bulk ingredient such as blackberries or in combination with elderberries or damsons.

Raspberries
High acid, relatively low tannin and pigment for a red winemaking ingredient. They tend to have a very strong flavour which may dominate the other ingredients. This flavour restricts the quantity which you may use to a maximum of two pounds of fruit to a gallon of any wine.

Red Currants
Usually used only in the production of rosé wines. Where this fruit is available, use at the rate of three pounds per gallon, with the addition of a 5ml teaspoonful of acid. Unless kept in the dark, rosé wines rapidly lose their colour. Even taking this precaution they still tend to have limited shelf lives and this wine is best drunk about six months after it has been made. Simply crush the fruit, place in the bucket with the other ingredients and ferment.

WHITE WINEMAKING INGREDIENTS

Apple

More problems are encountered with apple wines than with any others. Whilst it is possible to make good apple wines, they tend to be the most difficult for a number of reasons. There is probably a greater difference between the varieties of apple than any other fruit. The variation in the amount of tannin is the most important as far as we are concerned, as it affects both the taste and the ability of the wine to clear. It is more than coincidence that bland apple wines tend to be cloudy. Because of the large number of varieties, and the various mixes used by winemakers, it is impossible to give exact and detailed instructions. Suffice it to say that you will almost certainly need to experiment with blends but the final result will be well worth it. With apples, more than any other fruit, it is essential that once you have found a variety which gives you a successful wine you continue to use it.

Another major problem is extracting the juice. The fruits tend to be too hard to process by a simple pressing. Enzyme treatment is possible and the fruit can be chopped and stored in the deep freeze allowing the ice crystals to breakdown the cells. If you did not use an enzyme as the basis of your method of extraction then it is essential to add pectic enzyme, both to increase the yield of juice and to aid clarification. Apple juice is very prone to atmospheric oxidation and the liquid should always be sulphited. Apple wines are best made as light table wines for which you will require about five pounds per gallon. Increase the vinosity by adding a litre of pure white grape juice. Apart from this adjunct apple is not a good mixer and does not tend to make good dessert wines. It may, however, be used to make an excellent sparkling wine.

Bananas

Usually used as an additive to provide body to the wine. Although a fairly strong flavoured wine can be made from three pounds of fruit - enjoyed by some people although it is an acquired taste. Bananas have a low acid and tannin content and the quantity used is restricted by the flavour. Use no more than a pound per gallon. The body-providing materials develops as the fruit matures. It is ideal for winemaking when fully ripe and the skins are turning brown. Weigh complete with the skins which should then be discarded. Remove any pieces of the fruit which have turned brown in colour, place in a strong polythene bag and leave in the freezer for three days. Add liquid to the fermentation bucket and allow to remain for a week before straining. There are alternative ways of preparing the fruit, including adding fresh to the must, or simmer with water and adding just the liquid to the must. Both these methods tend to result in a strong banana flavour. The sugars contained within bananas are amongst the first to caramelise, and whilst this blends well with dessert wines, the presence of bananas is readily detectable and detracts from lighter wines.

Gooseberries

A very important ingredient for making white wines. Unfortunately insufficient attention has been paid to two important details in the past - the degree of ripeness of the fruit and the variety. Whilst all gooseberries harvested at any stage of maturity will give a reasonably drinkable wine, some retain an almost earthy gooseberry taste. For this fruit to reach its full potential, first choose the variety then wait until fully ripe, but before it has had the chance to begin to break down. Varieties to plant for winemaking include 'Keepsake', 'Lancer' and 'Leveller' the last of which is probably the best. When ripe they are of moderately high acidity and medium tannin, a fruit which can be used for all types of wines including sparkling. Use four pounds of fruit for a table wine and six for a gallon of dessert. Table wines tend to be at their best after six months to a year and desserts after two years.

White Currants

For a sweet after dinner white wine there is no better ingredient than white currant. It yields a rich full bodied wine without a hint of cloying. It is best used to make a sweet wine of between 12-14 per cent alcohol. Use four pounds per gallon and the only adjuncts which should ever be added is a white grape juice concentrate or sultanas. Always employ the cold method with sodium metabisulphite at all stages to protect the colour and prevent oxidation. When looking for an ingredient for sweet white wines in the British climate white currants are vastly superior to grapes. A must for every winemaker's garden, choose the variety 'White Versailles'.

Rhubarb

It might seem surprising to see rhubarb listed under fruit. For winemaking purposes it is usually classified as such, but before showing any rhubarb wines always check with the schedule. In some shows rhubarb is still accepted as a vegetable, which is hardly fair as it is vastly superior to any other vegetable as a winemaking ingredient. Rhubarb with its fresh, clean sharp taste is amongst the most versatile of winemaking materials, it can be used to make a sweet light table wine, or a heavier social wine. It is a great mimic, incorporated with other ingredients it soon takes on their characteristic making it ideal for blending - to raise acidity - or for topping up other wines. Rhubarb gathered before the end of July tends to make better, far less acidic, wines than that harvested late in the season. Strange folksy ways of making the wine abound but the modern method is easy. Use only the stalks which owe their acidity to malic acid. Under no circumstances should the leaves be used as they contain relatively large amounts of the poisonous acid oxalic, and when eaten have been known to kill people. Take the stalk and, without peeling, cut into pieces about two inches long. Place in a strong polythene bag and allow to stand in the freezer for a week before transferring to the fermentation bucket where it should be allowed to remain for a further week. The basic recipe, which consists of three pounds of rhubarb together with a litre of grape juice concentrate, is an excellent base for flower wines. Young rhubarb wines tend to be very sharp, but the ingredient ages far slower than others and it is more difficult to tell the age.

Stone Fruit
The most important of the stone fruits are plums and gages. Their low to medium acidity allows you to use up to five pounds a gallon to make a full bodied drink with a very distinctive plummy flavour - another acquired taste with no commercial equivalent, it definitely improves with keeping and should not be drunk until at least two years

old. Peaches and apricots are other examples of fruits which suffer from being strongly flavoured. Enjoyable in small amounts, large quantities tend to be overpowering. Restrict the use to three pounds per gallon and include two pounds of sultanas. These produce very distinctive novelty wines which are very popular for drinking after dinner. Cherries are similar, although many varieties are of higher acid, one pound of cherries can be added to a range of red and white wines in order to give it a more complex flavour and bouquet. With many stone fruits it is virtually impossible to remove the stone from the flesh. The most effective way of treating the fruit is to make a circular cut around the stone, this will be sufficient to facilitate the removal of the useful components during fermentation.

Citrus fruits
Three citrus fruits are important in winemaking, grape-fruit, Seville oranges and dessert oranges. The first two are used in making aperitifs, the latter a social style wine. Grapefruit are very high acid fruits, the most economical and practical way to make the wine is to use two litres of juice with two litres of grape juice, feed and try to fer-ment out an additional two and three quarter pounds of sugar, which will give a high alcohol astringent aperitif excellent for stimulating the appetite. The segments from three pounds of Seville oranges, together with a pound of sultanas, yields a wine with a well developed flavour - another excellent aperitif quite unlike anything available commercially. Neither grapefruit nor Seville oranges make good adjuncts for other ingredients. Dessert oranges are high in acid, and two litres of juice together with a litre of

white grape juice concentrate will make a gallon of a social wine which retains much of the flavour of the fresh fruit. In traditional country winemaking, oranges were used to replace lemons to provide some of the acidity and a slightly different flavour, and is used in the most popular dandelion wine recipe in this way.

DRIED FRUIT

Several different types of fruit are dried and available from homebrew or health food shops. Usually they contain about fifty percent sugar, a large amount of fibre together with other insoluble materials such as seeds and skin. They provide the wine with some sugar, body, flavourings and variable, but usually small, quantities of acid. Dried fruit are exceptionally good at developing vinosity. As a result of the drying process pectin will have been released and it will be necessary to treat with pectic enzyme wherever dried fruit has been used. The most important dried fruits for winemaking in addition to those described above are:

Apricots

Available in two grades, very light coloured usually as a result of treatment with sulphur dioxide to stop browning. These may be incorporated in both light table wines and fuller desserts to a maximum of one pound per gallon. A darker form in which the sugars have oxidised is only suitable for use in dessert wines.

Figs

The ones sold in slabs are the most practical and economic form to use. These contain maderised and heavily oxidised sugars and invariably result in a tawny coloured wine. They are only suitable for sherry type wines or rich dark madeira style desserts. Use no more than a pound per gallon. Do not use fresh figs as these give very disappointing results.

Peaches
Similar to apricots, but the quantities should be limited to half a pound per gallon for table wines and twice this quantity for dessert wines, as in larger quantities the flavour tends to be overpowering.

Prunes
These have a well developed taste, the result of the natural flavour of the plum and the drying effect of the sun upon the sugars. The ideal ingredient for inclusion in a sweet or cream sherry must at the rate of a pound per gallon; a half of this amount can be used in the maderised dessert style.

Dried *rose hips* are also available, their main contribution to a wine is body. They can be used at the rate of half a pound per gallon in sweet sherry types, maderised desserts, and tawny wines. Unfortunately they bestow a very characteristic taste on the wine which is not to everyone's liking.

Dried *sloes* can be obtained, but their only role is to provide tannin, with very limited amounts of acid, sugars, and body forming ingredients. Not recommended.

Dried *elderberries* provide a wine with tannin and little else. Far better to gather the fruit during September and October and store the excess in the deep freeze for use throughout the year.

Note. When using dried fruit you should usually include only one type in any particular wine and the quantities given are the maximum amount of dried fruit to use.

FLOWERS

Flowers provide only bouquet and flavour, nothing else, to the wine. Unlike fruit we do not expect the aroma of the flowers to change as the wine matures. The fragrance is at its optimum when put into the wine, gradually diminishing its intensity with time. What you smell on the bush is what you get in the wine.

It is widely agreed that there are only two flowers suitable for making the highest quality wines.

Elderflower

Do not believe those people who tell you that elderflower is not a good winemaking ingredient. Once very popular, it is now no longer in fashion, but since when was fashion a good judge of taste? The fragrance of elderflowers varies considerably from the sweet almost banana style bouquet which we are seeking, to a catlike acridity which should be rejected. Before harvesting carefully smell the flowers, delaying gathering until you find the scent you require. Never use any flowers whose smell you do not like, it will not improve in the wine. To make a flower wine - where the fragrance of the flower is the chief characteristic - use the petals from six to twelve medium sized flower heads. Additionally three to five heads can be incorporated in a variety of white table wines to provide bouquet where it is lacking.

Rose Petals

The other flower which can successfully be used to flavour wines is the rose. One of the oldest of food additives it was originally known as 'Roses of Attar' or the druggist rose, and was used extensively in Middle Eastern cookery for such delicacies as Turkish Delight. There is a tremendous variation in the intensity of bouquet between the types of roses and you will need to ascertain the exact quantity of petals to use. This will vary between one and two pints per gallon depending upon the fragrancy of the particular type of rose. Some of the 'old roses' and species roses are ideal for winemaking and are deserving of more attention.

VEGETABLES

Parsnips

This is the most important of all the vegetable ingredients due to the flavouring of the root providing the wine with a sherry like character. Parsnips should be used at the rate of three pounds to the gallon. The roots require boiling for half an hour in two pints of water and only the liquid used for compounding the must. This will result in small quantities of starch entering the liquid which would cause a haze. Break down the haze by the addition of the starch enzyme amylase at the same stage as the yeast.

Carrots

Can be used to make a traditional country wine which has a pronounced flavour. Well made it is an extremely worthwhile wine.

Swedes, turnips and *mangolds* have all been used for

winemaking but they tend to make drinks with an earthy flavour. *Pea pods* and *beans* provide a limited amount of body and little else and are all best avoided.

HERBS

Herbs have been used for centuries in winemaking, mainly to conceal the taste of off flavours produced by spoilage yeasts. Generally they have no place in modern winemaking. The major exception being vermouth mixtures based on wormwood. Such mixtures may be bought from any good homebrew supplier. They can be added to a grape juice concentrate, sultana or rhubarb base - the latter is particularly good yielding a top quality aperitif.

EQUIPMENT

Much of the equipment - spoons for stirring, measuring jugs and jelly bags - that you need for winemaking you will already have in your kitchen. But there are certain items which you will also need to purchase. Winemaking apparatus should be made from stainless steel, food grade plastic or glass. Never use aluminium, copper or other metal utensils as the metal can be leached out by the acid and the wine may be poisonous.

Where necessary purchase specially designed equipment from a homebrew shop. The main items which you will require to commence winemaking are:

1. Fermentation bucket, made from white plastic.

2. Wine Press - not essential for all types of wine. You will be able to make several without it but is extremely useful for berry fruits.

3. Funnels, straining or jelly bags.

4. Measuring cylinder.

5. Demijohns and airlocks.

6. Fermentation mat, belt or fermentation cabinet - to maintain the correct temperature. This may be unnecessary if you can find a position where there is a suitable temperature in one of the rooms of the house.

7. Racking tube - for syphoning clear liquid from the sediment - can be part glass, part plastic or all plastic.

8. Wine bottles - an adequate supply may be obtained from most restaurants.

9. Corks - use plastic covered flanged corks. These are less trouble than the barrel type corks and have the advantage that they are reuseable.

ESSENTIAL WINEMAKING AIDS

1. Sodium metabisulphite or campden tablets.
2. Pectic enzyme (pectolase) and starch enzyme (amylase).
3. Yeast nutrient.

DESIRABLE BUT NOT ESSENTIAL AIDS

1. Hydrometer.
2. Acid testing kit.

4: MAKING THE WINE

Wine is one of the few foods or drinks prepared for us by a living organism - other examples include cheese and yoghurt. Conditions which favour the growth of one type of organism will almost always support others, some of which will have harmful effects - in our case on the wine. Alcohol is a food for some of these organisms and may be destroyed; off flavours can develop which might render the liquid undrinkable. Such organisms can enter the liquid at any stage and once they have got into the wine it is seldom possible to effectively control them. By maintaining sterile conditions at all stages of the wine's manufacture and storage it is possible to control their entry.

The organisms which cause the problems lurk invisibly all around, on the surfaces of fruit, equipment that we use, work tops and are transported in the air. Your carefully prepared must or wine is constantly under threat. You must ensure that they are not on the ingredients or equipment at the start of the operation and be constantly on your guard so that they do not enter the liquid at any stage.

Cleaning alone is not enough, invisible wine germs will survive unless the surfaces are correctly treated. Sterilising equipment is easy, combined sterilising and cleaning powders are available from your homebrew shop which, providing they are used according to the manufacturer's instructions, will ensure all utensils are germ free. However, there is far more likelihood of germs being on the surface of ingredients and sterilising these is not so simple. The chlorine based chemicals used for sterilising equipment must not be used and alternative approaches are required.

The Hot Method
This consists of covering the fruit with boiling water. It is not the best method for most white wines or light bodied wines of any colour as inevitably there is a slight degree of caramelisation in the process; the method offers no protection against atmospheric oxidation, and many of the flavour providing esters and essential oils are volatilised off and lost. But it is very effective and has little detrimental effect on strong flavoured wines and many of the heavy dessert wines which take on a degree of oxidation in the maturation process. Country wines are most frequently made by the hot method and are extensively discussed in *Winemaking Month By Month*.

The Cold Method
In this method the fruit is treated with sodium metabisulphite, either as a solution of the powdered chemical or as campden tablets. The acidity of the must releases sulphur dioxide contained within the sodium metabisulphite. This kills bacteria and at the same time offers chemical protection against atmospheric oxidation. Sulphur dioxide can be used in winemaking because it

will gradually disperse in the liquid once its work is done. It is a reducing agent whose action is opposite to that of an oxidising material. It uses its reducing power to bleach materials, but unlike chlorine which is an oxidising bleach, once the sulphur dioxide has dissipated dissolved oxygen may reverse its affects. When metabisulphite is added to a red wine must there may be an initial loss of colour due to this reduction, but the colour gradually returns as the sulphur dioxide loses its potency. Sulphur dioxide can be used as an alternative method of sterilising equipment, which must first be thoroughly washed as the chemical has no detergent properties. To sterilise equipment keep a special bottle of 10% stock solution for this purpose. Pour the liquid in the utensils, or place the utensil in a fermentation bucket and add the liquid. Cover the container and leave for half an hour. Return the sulphite solution, which will still be active, to the stock bottle for use on future occasions.

Whenever sodium metabisulphite is used, it is as a 10% solution prepared by dissolving 10 grams of sodium metabisulphite in 100ml of water and keep stored in a stoppered bottle.

Providing the yeast
Yeast may be purchased in two forms, as a liquid culture or dried. Yeast should be stored in a cool dry place. Once the container has been opened all the yeast should be used. The exception is the drums of dried general purpose wine yeast which contain sufficient material to make several gallons. The combined effect of time, damp and warmth will result in the yeast losing its ability to reactivate.

Where yeast has been open for some time you can test

if it is still viable by taking one of the granules and placing it in the palm of your hand. Press the yeast with your finger. If it is still hard it is probably safe to use, but if it disintegrates into a powder the yeast will be dead!

Yeast Starters

To understand the role of a yeast starter it is necessary to realise that sulphur dioxide only suppresses living organisms. When confronted with a vigorously growing culture the chemical is impotent against it. The result is that the yeast will continue to grow in the presence of the chemical and its competitors are suppressed. If the yeast were not reactivated in this way, it would experience difficulties in growing in the presence of the sulphur dioxide and not regain its activity until the chemical had lost its potency, at which stage the other micro organisms present could similarly start growing again.

The day before you intend to make wine reactivate the yeast. Into a sterilised milk bottle place a solution of one tablespoonful of sugar dissolved in half a pint of water to which a quarter of a teaspoonful of citric acid has been added. Put a level 5ml teaspoonful of dried yeast into the liquid. Cover the top of the bottle with cling film and allow to stand at the fermentation temperature of 18.5-21C (65-70F).

Extracting the Juice

Wines are made from liquids not solids.

Whilst the newly formed alcohol will dissolve some flavourings out of solid plant materials, the quantities are small. It is the liquids of the fruits themselves which contain the materials which we need to make top quality wines.

Unless the liquid is efficiently extracted much of the fruit will be wasted. Many devices and methods of extracting juices have appeared on the market over the years, but two of the most effective methods are squeezing the juice out by using a fruit press or placing the fruit in the deep freeze. In the freezer ice crystals form within the fruit cells, and, as the temperature rises on thawing, the crystals expand, burst the cell walls, and the liquid runs out. Even if there appears to be very little liquid place this with the fruit in the fermentation bucket. The remaining liquids will be more readily released from the fruit after it has been frozen. But be aware that freezing will not kill wild yeasts and spoilage organisms. You must still sterilise fruit after it has been placed in the freezer. Other methods of breaking up the fruit such as food mixers can be very effective. But care should be taken with high tannin fruits such as elderberry, as they will macerate the astringent skins and the resultant wines will take several years to mellow.

When dealing with small quantities of fruit, such as that required to make a gallon of wine, it is often possible to extract the juice by hand squeezing through muslin or by chopping into small pieces.

Dried fruit should be cut in half to aid the extraction of the sugar and flavourings which they possess.

COMPOUNDING THE MUST

Before using the fermenting bucket make sure that the level of liquid which corresponds to a gallon of liquid is clearly marked - if necessary measure a gallon of water into the container and mark its position on the outside.

Place the fruit juices, any fruit to be fermented in the presence of the juice, together with the dried fruit, in the bucket.

The Quantity of Sugar

As we have seen, the alcoholic strength of a wine is directly related to the quantity of sugar which has been fermented, and we need to know approximately how much sugar to add to the must.

The amount of sugar in the ingredients can vary considerably from very little up to fifty percent of the weight with some dried fruit. The more solids dissolved in the liquid the greater will be its density. Since sugar is the only substance likely to be present in sufficient quantities to affect the density of the liquid, if we can determine the density then we will know how much sugar is present and how much we will need to add to raise it to a set level. Density is measured by means of an hydrometer.

An hydrometer is a hollow glass tube weighted at one end so that it floats upright in a liquid. In liquids which contain very little dissolved sugar the instrument will almost sink, with only the top of the tube not submerged, whereas with a solution which contains a large quantity of sugar virtually all of the tube floats. The instrument is calibrated by marking the position at the top of the tube in a liquid of known low density such as water and the position at the bottom in a concentrated sugar solution of known high density. The space in between is then divided equally to give the calibration. Should you ever need to check the accuracy of your instrument you can do this by placing it in water which has a specific gravity of 1.000. The specific gravity above 1.000 is due almost entirely to fermentable sugars, but as these are converted to alcohol the density of the liquid may fall below 1.000 as the solution is now mainly a mixture of water and alcohol. The latter when pure has a specific gravity of only 0.800. To use the hydrometer, pour some of the must into an hydrometer pot, taking care to include the minimum amount of air bubbles which would make the liquid buoyant yielding a false result. Give the hydrometer a gentle spin and read the calibration where the instrument come to rest. The liquid appears to rise up the stem of the instrument, the correct specific gravity is obtained by reading the level where the surface of the liquid just meets the stem.

The gravity will vary according to temperatures. Usually hydrometers are calibrated at 15C (59F). Variations of temperature of 5C (9F) above or below this figure - which covers the temperatures at which you are most likely to be working - will not adversely effect your measurements. Avoid determining the gravity of the liquid when the deviation is far greater than this amount if possible. Where measurements are taken outside of the recommended range it will be necessary to provide a temperature correction.

SPECIFIC GRAVITY TEMPERATURE CORRECTIONS

Temperature		Specific Gravity
C	F	Correction to be applied
5	41	-0.002
10	50	-0.001
15	59	+0.000
20	68	+0.001
25	77	+0.002
30	86	+0.003

Interpreting Hydrometer readings

The quantity of non-fermentable material is insignificant and may be ignored, the hydrometer reading is a measure of the amount of sugar present. If the hydrometer reading is 1.050 it means that the liquid contains the equivalent of 610 grams per 4.5 litres of sugar (see table below). If you require a gravity of 1.100 which corresponds to a total sugar level of 1205 grams (in 4.5 litres) you will need to add 1205-610 = 595 grams of sugar.

Working in the Imperial System for the same solution the calculation becomes: an hydrometer reading of 1.050 corresponds to 22oz per gallon. To produce a gravity of 1.100 which requires 43oz per gallon you will require an additional 21oz of sugar. Dissolve the sugar in the minimum amount of water and add to the bucket.

The potential alcohol concentrations are theoretical figures for the most efficient conversion of sugar to alcohol. In reality you are likely to obtain slightly lower results due to the variable effects of the inefficient aerobic fermentation. Allowing this to proceed for longer than is necessary burns up extra sugar; losses at the racking stage can also result in reduced yields. Alcohol figures nearer to the theoretical values will be obtained if an additional 2oz per gallon (50g/4.5 litres) is added to the musts for preparing 12% wines and twice this amount for 16% wines where the inefficiency is often higher.

Two pounds of sugar will dissolve in a pint of water and the solution will then occupy a total of two pints (1kg in 0.6 litres occupying 1.2 litres). Usually it is not necessary to make the solution as concentrated as this but you will need to restrict the quantity of water so that you will be able to get all of the liquid into the demijohn. Excess wine must is always wasted and should wherever possible be avoided. Add extra water if necessary to bring the level up to one gallon (4.5 litres). Additions after this stage will be insufficient to have a significant effect on the volume.

Specific gravity	Weight of Sugar oz/gal	g/4.5ltr	Potential Alcohol (% alcohol by volume)
1.030	13	380	5
1.040	18	500	6.5
1.050	22	610	8.0
1.060	26	735	9.5
1.070	30	850	11
1.080	34	970	12.5
1.090	38	1090	14.5
1.100	43	1205	16.0
1.110	47	1330	17.0
1.120	52	1445	19.0

Note these figures refer to a sugar contained in a solution made up to a gallon, not the quantity of sugar to which a gallon of water is added. The figure for potential alcohol is purely theoretical, no more than an indication. Actual percentages are almost always lower.

Acidity Correction
A good recipe will provide sufficient acid for the fermentation to proceed smoothly and for the wine to clear. Corrections, should they prove necessary, can always be performed following palate tests on the finished wine. If you are producing your own recipes or you wish to check the acidity at this stage, determine the value by following the

instructions provided on the acid testing kit, and any adjustments necessary can be made to increase or reduce the acid level.

To increase the acid level, either use citric acid crystals or to increase the vinosity as well a mixture of 50% tartaric acid, 30% citric acid and 20% malic acid. You will need to purchase the three acids separately. They should be thoroughly mixed and stored in a container with a tight-fitting non-metallic lid. Addition of a quarter ounce of either the pure citric acid or the mixture will raise the acidity of a gallon by one part per thousand (1 ppt) (7 grams raise the acidity of 4.5 litres by the same amount).

Reducing the acidity of the solution should not be necessary and you should always try to avoid the problem by using less fruit. Where it is necessary to lower the acidity a quarter ounce of precipitated chalk will, when added to a gallon, lower the acidity by 1.5 ppt.

Sterilising the Ingredients

Ingredients can be sterilised by sodium metabisulphite. Prepare a 10% stock solution by dissolving 2 ounces of sodium metabisulphite in a pint of water (50 grams in 500ml). Stored in a tightly stoppered bottle the solution will last for six months. Sterilise the ingredients by the addition of 5ml of a stock solution to a gallon of must. Alternatively you may use a crushed campden tablet per gallon. With fruit which tends to oxidise readily, or which is overripe and likely to be more heavily contaminated, you may use double this quantity - this additional amount is included in those recipes where it is considered necessary. Do not be tempted to use larger amounts as the heavier the sulphiting the more difficult it will be for the wine yeast to establish itself in the must.

Provide pectic enzyme, pectolase, which is required to break down any pectin present, to stop haze formation and help with the release of the juices still contained within the fruit tissue. Pectic enzyme is most effective when added at this stage. Being a delicate chemical it is destroyed by boiling water. Where starch is liable to be a problem, usually only with root wines, amylase should also be added at this stage.

Cover the bucket and allow to stand for 24 hours at fermentation temperature - 18.5-21C (65-70F). During this period the sulphur dioxide liberated will suppress wild yeast cells and spoilage organisms present, but it will not destroy them completely and unless you add the active yeast starter exactly one day after the addition of the sodium metabisulphite the harmful organisms will begin to recover, take over and destroy the liquid. It should stressed that the addition of sulphur dioxide to a must is not a method of preserving the liquid, but a means of creating optimum conditions which gives your chosen strain of yeast an unfair advantage to establish itself first and then take over to the exclusion of the other species.

Yeast Nutrient

The final additive to include at this stage is yeast nutrient. For rapid ferments or high alcohol wines we are seeking to encourage the yeast to perform at its absolute limits. To do this we must provide all of the nutrients which the yeast requires. A modern yeast food is complex and includes traces of vitamins which are essential to the plant as well as minerals. Add only the recommended quantity of nutrient - there is no advantage in increasing the amount, which apart from being wasteful, may leave a slightly salty taste in the finished wine.

STARTING THE FERMENTATION

A day after preparing the must add the by now vigorously working starter bottle. During the next one to two days the yeast will acclimatise itself to the new conditions and go through a new lag phase to be quickly superseded by vigorous activity as it enters the logarithmic stage. During this time the yeast needs maximum air dissolved in the water. The winemaker can help the process along by stirring the liquid daily to dissipate the carbon dioxide produced and to simultaneously help more air enter the must. Usually it takes about seven days for this vigorous phase to be complete, but it will vary depending upon the amount of sugar that is present and the temperature. Other factors, such as the size of the bucket and the amount of air above the liquid will all have an influence on the time taken to complete this stage. Times given in recipes can never be any more than an indication. Look at the surface of the liquid, when the vigorous activity begins to subside it is a sure sign that the logarithmic phase has ceased, the yeast is entering the steady state and must be immediately transfered to the demijohn.

TRANSFERING THE LIQUID TO THE DEMIJOHN

Where there is no solid material in the must the liquid may be decanted into the demijohn, and the residue already beginning to collect at the bottom of the bucket can be discarded. Where there is solid material present the liquid should be strained through muslin or a jelly bag. A gentle squeezing at this stage will ensure that the final traces of juice leave the solid material. If necessary, top up to just below the neck of the demijohn with water and fit an airlock.

Anaerobic fermentation resulting in maximum alcohol production will now occur and its progress can be monitored by the escape of the bubbles of carbon dioxide through the airlock. The gas production rate will gradually drop and the liquid become clearer, by which time a layer of solid material will have formed at the bottom of the demijohn. The liquid must be separated from this material which, if left, will be broken down by the enzymes of decay causing the wine to acquire a musty taste.

RACKING THE WINE

Racking consists of syphoning the liquid from the solid deposit at the bottom of the demijohn. This is easily done by placing the full demijohn on the work bench and a clean sterilised demijohn on the floor or at a more suitable height. A racking tube is placed in the top container, the liquid is sucked into the tube and a finger placed over the end to stop it escaping or air entering the tube. Remove your finger from the tube and place in the lower demijohn. The trap at the end of the racking tube will stop the solid material from passing into the new container. Discard the solid material and the small amount of liquid associated with it. If the wine is dry at this stage, after transfering to another demijohn, top up with water and cork. If the wine is still sweet, top up with water or pure grape juice to increase the vinosity, refit the airlock and allow fermentation to proceed. Gradually the precipitate will start to build up again. After a further six weeks, or when there is 3mm (1/8 in) of sediment, rerack the wine, topping up again. Usually two rackings are sufficient. The wine should have finished working and be clear at this stage, although dessert and other high alcohol wines may require an extra racking. After the final racking top up with water or grape juice and cork.

STORING WINE

Prior to storing you may treat by adding 5ml of 10% sodium metabisulphite solution, this will stop atmospheric oxidation and protect the colour of the wine. Unfortunately the dry harsh taste of sulphur dioxide may remain on the wine and detract from it. Although this procedure is widely recommended, the winemaker is advised to try unsulphited and sulphited wines and decide for himself which he prefers. Is the slight, often imperceptable, oxidation not preferable to the cure?

And remember the sulphur dioxide liberated does not offer complete protection against attack by spoilage organism, it simply makes it more difficult for them to grow. It is not a substitute for continued vigilance and good hygiene.

Sweet wines

Apart from dessert wines, or other maximum alcohol wines, if you add sugar the wine will usually start refermenting, become unstable, and remain so until all of the sugar has worked out leaving a dry wine once again. To overcome the problem either use one of the non-fermentable wine sweeteners on sale at homebrew shops or, if providing extra sugar, add both sodium metabisulphite (5ml of a stock solution or 1 campden tablet) and 1 gram of potassium sorbate (all quantities per gallon or 4.5 litres). Make sure that you do not omit the sodium metabisulphite or the wine will develop a geranium taste.

CLARIFICATION OF WINE

Correctly made wines from well balanced must should not normally require clarification. The vast majority will clear naturally and need no further treatment. The tannins, proteins and other materials will form giant heavy molecules which will precipitate out leaving you with a crystal clear liquid. But even the best winemakers experience cloudy wines from time to time and it is necessary to deal with them. They are the result of large particles being held in suspension in the liquid and the suspension must be broken down. The first advice if you have an unclear wine is be patient, allow sufficient time for natural clarification to occur, three months after fermentation has ceased should be long enough. But if the wine remains cloudy there is a possibility that it will not clear naturally. The old winemaking maxim of 'Allow the wine long enough to stand and the problems will go away' is definitely not true. Keeping a bad wine will only make it worse, as the suspensions cause problems far beyond the appearance of the liquid. Prolonged storage of an unclear wine can cause off flavours to develop as the solid materials held in suspension begin to break down. Moreover unclear wines are usually chemically unsound, often lacking acid or tannin, and a deficiency of the former can leave the liquid more liable to attack by bacteria.

The reasons for treating a wine to clear it go far beyond visible appearance and include:

1. removal of suspended matter.

2. removal of pigment, such as the slight traces of red, which can enter a white wine due to small quantities of colour in the skins of some fruits, such as certain varieties of gooseberries.

3. removal of some off flavours.

Before embarking on finings two very simple treatments are often effective. If the wine lacks tannin, as may be revealed by the taste, extra should be added. Or place the wine, with or without the addition of extra tannin, outdoors on a frosty night. The sudden drop in temperature is often sufficient to precipitate the suspended material. But if this is unsuccessful you will have to use finings.

Fining

Fining is clarifying wine by adding a material which reacts with a chemical in the wine or one added to it, usually tannin although it may be acids or protein, to form a giant molecule which entraps suspended matter. Experience shows that high acid and/or high tannin wines can be more successfully fined than those low in these components. Traditional methods include the addition of blood and skimmed milk, neither of which can be recommended. Many finings are protein based - gelatin, isinglass, chitin as well as the acidic tannin and the inorganic bentonite. Several commercially available fining agents are based on these materials. Because of the many and varied compositions of wines it is not always possible to say which fining agent will be the most successful and there will be times when a degree of trial and error will be involved. Try small scale tests to see which method is likely to prove successful rather than subject the wine to a barrage of clarification procedures.

Bentonite

This is a type of clay, the dried form of which swells enormously when water is added. It is found mainly in an area of Wyoming. The degree of success varies with the wine and it is not always possible to predict when it will solve the problem. Bentonite has the advantage that it leaves virtually no detectable taste. Take a teaspoonful of bentonite, add twice its volume of water, and allow to stand overnight. In the morning you should have a thick paste. Shake this with about half a pint of wine until it is evenly distributed, then add to the remainder of the gallon of wine (or less if it is impractical because of the size of the vessel). Thoroughly shake for ten minutes. An arm aching task but it is necessary to thoroughly distribute the material. An activated form of bentonite, in which the clay is made up into a gel, is available and is easier to use.

Gelatin

This is extracted from bones, being obtained from the natural connective tissue of mammals. Gelatin for wine clearing is purchased as thin sheets. Prepare a one percent solution by warming the gelatin in a small quantity of wine and then adding to the wine. Gelatin is only successful if there is sufficient tannin present. If low levels are expected from taste assessment tests additional tannin should be added to the wine forty eight hours before the gelatin.

Isinglass
This is obtained from the swim bladder of sturgeons and tends to be expensive. It is used in a similar manner to gelatin. Again extra tannin may be required.

Egg albumen
Once the traditional clearing agent for wines, in recent years it has fallen from favour. The main problem is keeping the quantities of albumen to a minimum. Twenty four hours before the wine is to be treated add a few drops of extra tannin solution. Shake a quarter of the white of an egg in half a pint of wine. Then add the whole to a gallon (or five gallons because even at this dilution there will be far more fining agent than is needed for the volume of wine) and shake thoroughly. Allow to stand for a fortnight.

Casein
Casein is the main protein of milk and if pure casein is not available you can use a small amount of dried milk. Casein itself is insoluble but will dissolve in bicarbonate of soda. Take half a teaspoonful of casein and a similar quantity of bicarbonate of soda and dissolve in a small quantity of water. Add to the wine. The acidity of the wine neutralises the bicarbonate causing the casein to form an even bulky precipitate which as it settles traps the suspended material. In addition to clearing it will decolourise pale rosé wines by absorbing pigment molecules.

Enzymes
Late additions of either pectic or starch (amylase) enzyme will in certain circumstances clarify the wine, but they

are only effective if the haze is due to the presence of pectin (found in most fruits) or starch usually only associated with root wines. The enzymes hydrolyse the large starch or pectin molecules, effectively breaking them down into units which are no longer a problem. This method is unlikely to be effective if enzymes were originally added at the same time as the yeast.

It is possible to buy the finings described above from good homebrew suppliers. There are proprietary finings on the market, some of which are variations on the materials listed and others which possibly employ different ingredients. Some are also available in prepared forms which make them far easier to use. It is probably possible to clear every wine, it is simply a matter of choosing the correct fining. When using any fining always follow the manufacturer's instructions carefully.

Charcoal
Active charcoal has the ability to absorb minute amounts of impurities, for which it is used extensively in the pharmaceutical industry. When added in small amounts it removes traces of off flavours from wines. However it will also remove delicate bouquet-producing materials should they still remain. Wines treated with this chemical, whilst being drinkable, tend to be dull and boring.

Filters
Wine filters will remove the final traces of suspended matter and produce a star-bright wine which seems to sparkle in the light. Filters are far more effective on wines which have at least partially cleared and you should never

pass a really cloudy wine through a filter. After using a filter, thoroughly clean and sterilise before storing.

Oak

The oakiness of a barrel definitely improves the character of some wines, and oak as chips may be added at the rate of one to two grams per gallon. After about a month there is often a perceptible darkening of colour and an almost instantly matured taste to several dessert wines. When making sweet sherry types it is usually preferable to add roast oak chips. Where oak is added it is necessary from time to time to sample the wine in order to establish when the 'barrel taste' is sufficiently well developed. Experience has taught the professional vigneron that wine can remain in the barrel for up to four years. It does not necessarily follow that this is the case with homemade wines because of the scale of operation. At home we are dealing with far smaller quantities and the amount of flavouring materials will depend to some extent on the ratio of surface area of the oak to the volume of liquid. Moreover we use fresh oak chips every time whereas the barrels of the vineyards tend to be many years old with much of the active flavouring long since leached out. For the amateur winemaker this is still a matter for experimentation.

A few drops of vanilla essence can be added to light red table wines to improve their character, but care must be taken as this is a flavouring which can easily dominate.

Storage of Wine

Except for certain light table wines, most wines benefit from a period of storage. During this time the alcohol and acids combine to form esters, slight oxidations occur from the small amount of dissolved oxygen, harsh substances undergo change, whilst tannins are precipitated from solution and the wine acquires an altogether more mellow flavour.

Wine requires an even storage temperature, lack of fluctuation is more important than exact value, but aim to keep the wine at or as near to 7C (45F) as possible. Always store wines out of direct sunlight and preferably in the dark. The energy of the sun's rays is sufficient to bring about chemical changes, most noticeably the breakdown of the pigment. Rosés soon become a dirty brown colour when stored in bright sunlight and whites similarly darken.

Wine must either be stored in full demijohns or bottled. Never draw wine for drinking directly from the demijohn. The air space which will form will cause rapid deterioration of the remaining liquid - possibly within a week.

One gallon of wine will yield six bottles.

When bottling wines you may reuse corks, but they can carry disease. Treat the corks by standing overnight in a sterilising solution made from a 10% solution of sodium metabisulphite solution and citric acid.

Records

To continually improve your wine it is useful to keep detailed records of each batch that you make for future reference. Make a note of the exact recipe, the starting date, and the time taken for each stage in the preparation process. Include details of specific gravities together with acid levels if measured.

Equally important are tasting notes. Record the age at which the wine was first, and subsequently, tasted and record your impressions on each occasion. Note any changes in colour, bouquet or flavour which can alter over the maturation stage so that you are better informed in the future as to the best time to drink the wine.

SUMMARY OF THE STEPS IN WINEMAKING

This is the general method to be used:

Day 1

1. Wash and sterilise all equipment. Rinse out with clean water.

2. Prepare starter bottle.

3. Prepare the fruit by extracting juices, chopping fruit and following other detailed instructions in the recipe.

4. Add sugar, any additional acid, together with pectic enzyme and/or starch enzyme and yeast nutrient. Make liquid up to one gallon.

Day 2

Add vigorously acting yeast starter. If the starter is not working this stage can be delayed for 48 hours but no longer. If the yeast starter is not working, and you have used the correct quantities of materials, the problem will either be that the temperature is wrong or that the yeast is dead. If the temperature was maintained at 70F + or - 5F (21C + or -3C), then use a fresh batch of yeast.

Days 3-14 (approx)

1. Stir the wine daily.

2. Study the vigorous head of bubbles forming on the

surface of the liquid. It will drop back to a steady production of carbon dioxide bubbles which, depending upon the yeast strain, temperature and quantity of sugar, can take from five to fourteen days from the time that the yeast was added.

3. As soon as the head has subsided to a steady bubbling, strain the liquid (if necessary) through muslin or a jelly bag and transfer to a demijohn.

4. Top up with water and fit an airlock.

Weeks 2-10

1. Watch the escape of gas from the airlock, when it has ceased or is imperceptibly slow the wine must be racked. This stage will also vary with the factors listed above. Delaying racking up to ten weeks from starting the wine should not cause problems.

If fermentation continues beyond this point it is a sign that your temperature is again too low.

2. Once activity has ceased, rack the wine. Taste or test with an hydrometer to ascertain the amount of residual sugar. If the wine is dry, top up with water, add a campden tablet or 5ml of a 10% solution of sodium metabisulphate, and place a cork in the demijohn.

If the liquid is still sweet, top up with sugar syrup or grape juice and allow to referment to dryness at which stage the wine should be reracked.

Top up the liquid with water for dry wines or grape juice for sweet wines. Allow to stand until clear.

When the Wine has cleared in the Demijohn
Bottle the wine, fit a cork and store in an even temperature.

If the wine is not clear three months after the final racking, treat with finings.

5: FAULTS AND DISORDERS

Providing that the procedures previously described are strictly followed you should not experience any problems with your winemaking. Many winemakers ferment for years without difficulties, producing gallon after gallon of successful brews. Nevertheless, problems can and do occur, especially if the winemaker allows his standards to slip.

Once faults have occurred it is seldom easy to cure them and it is often necessary to pour the contaminated liquid down the sink. It is this waste and disappointment, coupled with a sense of almost inevitability, which has so often discouraged people from making wines in the past. This is a pity because with a little understanding all problems are totally avoidable.

Should a fault occur it is necessary that you can identify it, understand what went wrong, and avoid the problem in the future. But do not let the faults and disorders deter you. The following is a list of virtually all the problems which could occur. The vast majority you will never experience and none of them will be a problem if you develop a good winemaking technique.

BIOLOGICAL FAULTS

These may result from three types of organisms:

1) Bacteria
2) Yeasts
3) Moulds

Bacterial faults

Bacteria are the simplest and most widespread of all cellular organisms. They are essential to life on this planet. Many are instrumental in the continuing natural recycling process by breaking down once living material. But the range of bacteria is enormous, with a few, the pathogens, producing toxins that cause food poisoning and which can bring about terrible diseases in humans and animals. Wine, and the must from which it is made, are the ideal mediums in which some bacteria can live and grow, providing adequate moisture, nutrients and the correct temperature range. And growth can be rapid under ideal conditions - a single bacterium will increase from one to over a million in just seven hours. Whilst such perfect conditions, from the bacteria's point of view, may not exist within the demijohn, massive increases in numbers will occur where wine stands undisturbed for several months.

Bacteria which affect wine often break down alcohol and other compounds to carbon dioxide and water, leaving a flat insipid drink with its protection reduced, and which is now open to attack by other organisms. Bacteria do not occur in nature in isolation and there are several species which prosper under the same conditions. Usually wine is destroyed by not one but several different bacteria working together. As one species breaks down the alcohol or acid it reduces the inborn protection to further bacterial attacks. Other forms which produce a variety of off flavours then start to grow. All organisms require some nutrients in small amounts in addition to their main food supply. In a winemaking situation spoilage organisms can often only obtain these extra nutrients when they are recycled by the break down of dead cells such as those which make up the lees. Wine which is unclear, or is standing on a sediment, will be attacked more quickly by spoilage organisms once infected and the damage will be far greater.

There are two main groups of bacteria which attack wines:

Lactobacilli

These are rod-shaped organisms that live and grow in the absence of air and that will attack the wine whilst it is in the demijohn. They are responsible for the conversion of acids and other compounds to lactic acid. These bacteria can cause a range of problems depending upon the species involved. Infected or sick wines exhibit a number of characteristic off flavours. It is not always possible to state whether they are due to lactobacilli or putrefication bacteria, although the latter tend to be associated mainly with wines which initially had a low acidity. Identifying the exact bacteria responsible for the problem is not as important as the ability to recognise the fault for what it is - the result of poor winemaking. Lactic acid bacteria can cause bitter or sour tastes to develop in the wine. It can be difficult to establish whether the taste has been caused through infection or the ingredient, especially where there is any possibility of the pith of citrus fruits or stalks entering the must.

A member of the lactobacillus group is thought to be responsible for the condition known as mouse in which the wine acquires a mousy taste and smell. Many winemakers experience difficulty recognising mouse. It is not immediately apparent, but a matter of seconds after swallowing the wine, a stale biscuit-like taste develops and lingers at the back of the throat reminiscent of the odour emitted by mice. Mouse is due to the presence of an alkaline substance which is only released when the acid of the wine has been neutralised by salivary juices, this accounts for the delay in its detection. If in doubt, there are two aids to its detection. A small quantity of the wine can be placed on the palm of the hand, the hands rubbed together and then smelt. The alkaline sweat always present on the surface of the skin will help aid its identification, but you should be careful where you perform the test as you will need to wash your sticky hands immediately afterwards. A more powerful aid to detection is to add bicarbonate of soda to the wine. There will be an immediate fizzing as the bicarbonate neutralises the acid, releasing carbon dioxide in the process. When no further effervescence occurs on the addition of extra bicarbonate the liquid will then be alkaline. If the liquid is then tasted and mouse is present it will be immediately obvious.

On tasting some infected wines there is a general condition known as sickness in which the liquid acquires a generally objectionable and unhealthy taste. Depending upon the exact nature of the taste this may be due to lactobacillus or putrefaction bacteria.

Acetobacter
These are the group of bacteria which require air and convert alcohol into acetic acid (vinegar), a biological

oxidation process. They produce the typical sharp taste of vinegar detected as a burning sensation at the back of the throat. Depending upon the exact type of bacteria, the length of time and the amount of air available the acetic acid may combine (esterify) with some of the available alcohol to form a series of acetates which have a characteristic smell (and taste to match) that ranges from peardrops to paint stripper. Acetic acid forming bacteria need high oxygen levels to grow and are only likely to occur when a demijohn is left half filled, or where quantities of wine-related liquids are allowed to remain in the bottom of containers. If a very small amount of wine is left standing in a large container it will in time form a white scum over the surface. This is due to the number of acetic acid forming bacteria becoming so large that, congregated together, they become visible to the naked eye. This liquid is known as the 'Mother of Vinegar' and used to be used as a starter for making vinegar. Acetobacter are tolerant of more acidic conditions than many bacteria but they do not grow significantly at pH values below 3. They seldom attack wines with an alcohol level above 13%. Once vinegaring has set in there is nothing that you can do to stop the process. Sulphur dioxide will control the bacteria's growth but will not remove the volatile acid which has already formed. As soon as vinegaring is suspected the wine should be destroyed immediately and a sterilising agent placed in the container. Acetobacter are not mobile but they are readily transported on air currents. Where infected liquids are allowed to remain exposed to the atmosphere for a prolonged period of time the air becomes supercharged with the bacteria as do all walls and surfaces, so aim to destroy the infected liquid as soon as it is noticed. One way that both fruit and liquids are frequently contaminated is by the fruit or vinegar fly *Drosophila melanogaster*. These tiny flies seem to appear as if by magic to hover within the vicinity of either fruit or wine during the autumn. Like most flies they eject gastric juices on to the fruit, semi-digest the food outside of their bodies and suck the nutrient rich liquid back into their stomachs. They then fly off to repeat the process elsewhere. Not surprisingly the vinegaring bacteria and other diseases are soon spread.

Putrefaction Bacteria and Food Poisoning

Lactobacillus and acetobacter are the only two major groups of bacteria encountered in a wine must, or the finished drink, because they are two of the relatively few classes capable of surviving in fairly strong acidic solutions. They will grow actively in solutions of pH 3-4 which is the typical acidity of a wine must, conditions which are hostile to most other micro-organisms.

The vast majority of bacteria, including those which are mainly responsible for food poisoning, grow most rapidly in neutral solutions (pH 7). They tend not to be able to survive in the acidic conditions tolerated by wine spoilage organisms, another reason why it is so important to ensure the correct degree of acidity. One type of spoilage often encountered in low alcohol and acid wines, particularly whites, and which may be due to putrefication bacteria is 'sickness', a condition in which the wine acquires an objectionable bouquet and taste which can be likened to fusty cheese, unwashed socks or, in extreme cases, urine. Another type of sickness results in a taste and bouquet similar to diesel oil. This seems to be particularly pronounced when an infected wine is treated with sulphur dioxide. Needless to say such wines must be immediately destroyed, and there should be a complete review of winemaking methods including reexamination of the recipes, as there may be insufficient acid to afford the wine the necessary protection.

Spoilage Yeasts

There are scientific differences between yeasts and bacteria. Bacteria grow by division of the nuclei, simply splitting into two, whereas yeasts form buds similar to the way in which some cacti grow. Bacteria, unlike yeasts, do not posses rigid cell walls. Yet the winemaker may be blissfully unaware that there are any differences at all as both grow in similar conditions; both have the ability to destroy the wine, albeit in different ways, and both are similarly controlled by sulphur dioxide. Only one species of yeast, *saccharomyces cerevisiae var. ellipsoideus,* is capable of creating a wine of the quality required. But, like bacteria, other yeast species are all around particularly on the skins of fruit. In wine growing districts there are a variety of wild yeasts, and usually more than one was involved in the traditional method of wine fermentation, which relied entirely upon natural yeasts. Success depended upon one species starting a rapid ferment and when it was no longer capable of growing in the alcoholic conditions that it had created another species would immediately take over. This produced adequate wines, and until we knew that there was a more reliable way, this was the only practical method available. Today the vast majority of grapes used in commercial winemaking are treated first with sulphur dioxide before an active yeast starter is added.

Allowing fermentation by wild yeasts present on the skins of the fruit, especially those other than the grape, is fraught with danger. Amongst the naturally occurring yeasts are some which will start fermenting very rapidly, but they are soon poisoned by low levels of alcohol, 4-5%. The initial, very vigorous, fermentation is accompanied often by various off flavours which detract from the quality of the wine. Where reliance is placed entirely upon wild yeasts there may be no species present capable of surviving the initial stage to take over and continue the process. The result will be a 'stuck' ferment, yielding a sweet cordial type drink containing very little alcohol and virtually no in built protection from other infections. Some wild yeasts will cause excessive ester production yielding strong flavours and others will increase the acidity of the wine. Much of the character of cider is developed as a result of a naturally present yeast which increases the acidity. Where apples are neither sulphited nor treated in other ways, wines with cidery tastes often result, irrespective of the variety of apple that was used.

A member of a non-alcohol forming group of yeasts, *Candida,* is responsible for 'Flowers of Wine'. This is a white film of yeast on the surface of a wine or must which has been exposed to the air for a considerable period of time. *Candida* yeast breaks the alcohol down to carbon dioxide and water.

Wild yeasts are far less tolerant than cultured yeasts to sulphur dioxide, which suppresses their growth and allows the desired form to become established and dominate the fermentation.

Medicinal taste

Another problem which can occur when musts contain insufficient acid is that the wine acquires a very distinctive and unmistakable medicine-like taste. There is little that can be done to retrieve the wine and it should be discarded.

Moulds

Moulds are the white, green or grey skins, or hairlike growths which tend to appear on a whole range of foods. Mould spores are everywhere and they will grow on any surface. Perhaps the most famous of all moulds is *Penicillium*, first found growing on bread and subsequently on fruits such as over ripe oranges. You are unlikely to experience major problems with moulds on wine although left exposed to the atmosphere it can happen. The main problem is the effect that the moulds have upon the fruit itself (page 52).

CHEMICAL FAULTS

Oxidation

Oxidation is the name given to a wide range of processes in which oxygen is added to other chemicals. The conditions which favour one type of oxidation will not necessary bring about other types. Bacteria will oxidise alcohol to acetic acid and even as far as carbon dioxide and water but, in the absence of living organisms, this process does not normally occur in a wine. A less drastic form of the oxidation of alcohol is the conversion of a small amount to acetaldehyde which will occur when a wine is left standing in the presence of excess air, or for prolonged periods in the presence of a limited air supply. The acetaldehyde imparts a distinctive flavour to the wine and whether this is beneficial or detrimental will depend upon the style of wine. Controlled oxidation to allow the formation of a small amount of acetaldehyde is one of the most significant chemical changes responsible for sherrying. This may be brought about by allowing a flor to develop and the wine then imitates the commercial method. This is unreliable for amateurs and it is better to stick to the controlled atmospheric oxidation of high alcohol wines. Acetaldehyde is overpowering in lighter wines and renders them undrinkable.

Some oxidation is inevitable. It is impossible to exclude air completely; it brings about changes in pigments, white wines gradually take on a slight brownish colour, reds lose their brightness and pass through a red golden stage. After many years of slow oxidation the reds acquire a tawny hue. Like the whites, whether or not a limited amount of oxidation is beneficial will depend upon the strength of the wine. The stronger a wine the more oxidation it can carry, but excess oxidation is always a fault.

Maderisation

This is the sweet, almost caramel, taste which one of the sugars in the wine, fructose, chemically breaking down. The process is accelerated by raising the temperature and madeira style wines may be deliberately stored at higher temperatures 45C (150F) for about three months to produce this effect. Keeping wines at lower temperatures for two or three years may have a similar effect. With both red and white sweet high alcohol wines this can greatly add to the character of the wine, and the home winemaker may find experiments in storing some of his dessert wines in warmer parts of the house very rewarding. As with sherrying, maderisation of light dry wines ruins them. Maderisation is due to the formation of hydroxymethylfurfural.

Sulphur Dioxide

We have already seen how useful sulphur dioxide is to the winemaker, but you can have too much of a good thing. Wines treated with sodium metabisulphite after the final racking will retain some of the active ingredient which gives a hot, dry, almost burning, sensation at the back of the throat. The effects of sulphur dioxide will gradually disappear, this is one of the few problems which will actually be solved simply by keeping the wine.

Hydrogen Sulphide

Very occasionally a wine develops the smell of hydrogen sulphide, bad eggs! Such wines must be immediately destroyed, they will get worse rather than improve and should never be drunk. The gas is very poisonous and the liquid should be disposed of out of doors. The hydrogen sulphide is produced as a result of the reduction of the sulphur dioxide to sulphur followed by further reduction by yeast to produce the poisonous gas. Whilst the exact mechanism and circumstances which lead to its development are not known, it is rare and is almost always the result of either bad winemaking or a poor recipe.

Ammonia

Ammonia and related compounds such as the amines which smell of decaying fish are rarely encountered in winemaking, but they can occur. They are the result of putrefication bacteria and only occur in low acidity musts which would almost certainly have failed for some other reason. Whenever any such strong smells are detected the wine must be discarded.

Peppery Taste and Smell

Some kit wines and others made using several different chemicals - yeast nutrient, clearing agent, potassium sorbate and sulphite - added in quick succession may, if drunk early, have a peppery taste. This taste which is totally harmless reflects the amount of chemicals which have been added. It will soon disappear.

Geranium

Sometimes wine acquires a geranium taste. This only occurs where potassium sorbate is incorrectly used to stabilise a wine. Whenever the chemical is added you must always provide a campden tablet or 5ml of a 10% solution of sodium metabisulphite.

TCP

Very occasionally wines acquire a pronounced TCP (Trichlorophenol) smell and flavour. More cases have been reported of it occurring in beer but it is sometimes found in wines. The phenols originate from the fruit. Mystery surrounds the source of the chlorine which may differ from winemaker to winemaker. One possible source of the chemical would seem to be from chlorine based cleaning and sterilising fluids or the old fashioned practice, now no longer recommended, of using bleach for sterilising equipment. If it is a problem, check that you are washing out thoroughly after sterilising, and try using sodium metabisulphite and citric acid as your sterilising agent. It has been suggested that it could be due to the presence of too much chlorine in the local water supply and so, if you still experience problems, check through the local wine circle or even a letter to the press to see whether other people suffer from TCP in their wine. If they are, it may be a problem of the district and therefore contact the local water board.

Colloidal Hazes

Pectin, starch and even dissolved metals (although these should never be encountered using modern food grade plastics) can form stable colloidal systems which stop a wine from clearing. These together with their treatment are discussed on page 78.

Woodiness

Pips of berry fruits such as blackberries and the stones of members of the Prunus family - damsons, plums, peaches, and apricots - can impart a woody taste to wine as a result of the alcohol leaching out materials from the seed casings. Avoid the problem in future years by separating and discarding the seeds before adding the fruit to the must, or in the case of small Prunus, such as cherries or sloes, remove the stones as part of the daily stirring routine when they become free of the flesh of the fruit.

Greenness, Stalkiness

The term 'green' is used to describe a young immature wine in which the acids are still sharp and it may still contain relatively large quantities of tannin in solution.

This problem is one which will disappear as the wine matures.

The word is also used in country winemaking to describe a drink which possesses the taste of green plant material. As this often originates from the stalks it is also referred to as stalkiness. In future brews ensure that you take the greatest care to remove all traces of greenery before placing the fruit or flowers in the fermentation bucket.

Stuck Ferments

These are the result of poor winemaking, where the yeast prematurely stops working, leaving only a sweet cloying liquid similar to a fruit cordial base. It can be due to the presence of too much sugar, using a poor yeast or too low a temperature. Such mixtures, which are usually stable to attack from spoilage organisms, can be saved by the doubling up technique. Prepare a yeast starter. When this is fermenting vigorously place it in a separate demijohn and add an equal volume of the stuck wine. Fit an airlock. When the mixture is again fermenting vigorously, add an equal volume of the stuck wine. Repeat the procedure until all the liquid has been transfered to the new demijohn. Once the wine has been restarted it is fermented out in the usual way.

Caution. Before deciding that a ferment is stuck always taste the wine and make sure that it is not dry. Sometimes wines ferment very quickly and the process is completed much earlier than was expected.

6: RECIPES

WINES FROM CONCENTRATES

Concentrates for winemaking vary considerably both in quality and in composition. The most popular are those based upon grape juice concentrate, but other fruits are used. Good wines can be made from concentrates and generally the more expensive products yield the better drinks. Some wines made from concentrates may be low in alcohol, but this can be overcome by initially adding one and a half times the amount of sugar recommended in the instructions. Assess the improvement and adjust the addition as necessary in the future. The main criticism is that wines made from concentrates tend to lack zest or freshness and the final product is bland compared with commercial wines. Increasing the alcohol will help lift the wine, and the inclusion of another ingredient which contains acid and tannin will complete the improvement.

The recommendations given below should be the basis of your initial attempts to improve the wine. Based upon the experience gained with a particular brand you can make further adjustments - but do not forget you may be able to achieve what you are seeking simply by purchasing a different concentrate in future.

IMPROVING WHITE TABLE WINES FROM CONCENTRATES

Method 1

To begin with make the wine according to the manufacturer's instructions. The easiest way to improve a white table wine is to replace a litre of water with a carton of pure grape juice. This will supply some extra sugar which may be sufficient to increase the alcohol.

Method 2

Take one pound of rhubarb, chop into pieces about two inches in length and allow to stand in the deep freeze for one week. Transfer the solid and any liquid which has flowed from the stems into the fermentation bucket. Sterilise by covering with two pints of boiling water. Allow to cool. Add the grape juice concentrate, together with the sugar (including any extra you may wish to add to raise the strength) and make up to one gallon. Add the vigorously working yeast starter. Strain after seven days and transfer to the demijohn.

Method 3

Take a pound of ripe gooseberries, crush and place in the fermentation bucket, add the grape juice concentrate, sugar dissolved in water (the recommended quantity plus any you wish to add) and make the whole up to one gallon. Add pectic enzyme and 5ml of a 10% solution of sodium metabisulphite or one crushed campden tablet. After twenty four hours add the vigorously working yeast starter. Strain after seven days and transfer to a demijohn.

Method 4
This is a variation on the above method but instead of using fresh gooseberries, replace them with a 400 gm can of the fruit. Since all the ingredients which are involved will be sterile there is no need to treat further. Place fruit, concentrate, sugar and pectic enzyme in the fermentation bucket. Make up to one gallon and add the yeast starter. Strain and transfer to the demijohn after a week.

A flowery bouquet can be added to a white grape juice concentrate wine using the technique described on page 113.

IMPROVING RED TABLE WINES MADE FROM CONCENTRATES

With this type of wine there is usually a need to increase the tannins and other materials which would be leached from the skin of the fruit by the newly formed alcohol if the fermentation had taken place in the presence of the grapes.

Take either

1lb (450g) Blackberries
or 12oz (350g) Loganberries
or 8oz (250g) Damsons
or 6oz (175g) Elderberries
together with a 5ml tsp of citric acid or acid mix

Place the fruit in the fermentation bucket - having crushed (or in the case of damsons cut) the fruit, together with the concentrate, the recommended quantity of sugar plus any extra you wish to add, and pectic enzyme. Make up to one gallon (4.5ltr) with water and add 5ml of a 10% solution of sodium metabisulphite or one campden tablet. After twenty four hours add the vigorously working yeast starter. Stir daily, after seven days strain and transfer to a demijohn.

IMPROVING DESSERT WINES MADE FROM CONCENTRATES

When dessert wines and sweet sherries are made from concentrates they invariably lack body and the most effective way to provide this characteristic is to include a pound (450g) of sultanas in each gallon of white wine or raisins in a gallon of red or tawny wine. This alone will improve the wine immeasurably - not only will the dried grape provide dissolved solids which increase the body, but also the sugar which they contain will increase the alcohol. The addition of a teaspoonful of glycerine per gallon of wine will help to increase the body of the wine and to give it a smoother finish. Alternatively sweet sherries, but not dessert wines, can be improved by the addition of half a pound (250g) of dried prunes or a one pound tin of the same fruit. Dry sherries can be improved by adding the liquid from boiling a pound of parsnips.

FRUIT WINES FROM CONCENTRATES

Country fruit winemaking concentrates are available, these may be based either on a grape juice concentrate to which the fruit has been added as a flavouring or on a non grape fruit base. Generally these kits contain sufficient flavour of the main fruit and there is little to be achieved by supplementing it. Usually the wines tend to be a little flat, lacking the zip of those made from fresh fruit and are low on body. As an initial approach to improving the wine add half a litre of grape juice and half a pound (250g) of sultanas.

With all concentrate wines, if you are seeking to improve them the secret lies in progressively trying small additions of acid and tannin (both of which can be added to the finished wine), extra sugar, extra fruit and dried fruit to provide more body.

WHITE DRY TABLE WINE

The ideal white table wine imparts a clear crisp taste. Its role is to clear the palate yet at the same time to possess such a delicate character that it will compliment, rather than compete with, mild flavoured foods such as fish and chicken. The bouquet may possess just a hint of floweriness as is naturally found in some grape varieties. This can be imparted to a homemade wine by including three medium sized elderflower heads in the recipe. The delicate character of white table wines means that the slightest imperfection is instantly detectable and you must take great care. Some commercial white table wines are below 12% alcohol but to make these in the home will cause problems as the wines do not possess the necessary keeping properties. Many so-called dry wines, especially those at the upper gravity limit, are only medium dry. This is usually perfectly acceptable with a meal, the slight amount of sugar may be sufficient to disguise a slight imperfection of flavour.

Ideal Starting gravity - 1.085-1.090
Finishing Gravity) 0.998-1.003
Alcohol Level 12-14%
Acidity 5-7 ppt

APPLE BASE

6lb (2.7kg) Apples
8oz (250g) Sultanas
2½lb (1.15kg) Sugar
Pectic Enzyme
Yeast Starter

Day 1

Remove stalks and any decay or damage from the apples, but do not peel, chop up and place in the fermentation bucket. Cut up the sultanas. Dissolve the sugar in water and add to the bucket. Make up to one gallon with water. Add 10ml of a stock solution of sodium metabisulphite or two crushed campden tablets. Add the pectic enzyme. Cover the bucket and allow to stand for a day. From now until fermentation is complete maintain the temperature at 18.5-21C (65-70F).

Day 2

Add the vigorously acting yeast starter. Stir daily.

Day 9

Strain, transferring to a demijohn. Occasionally apple wines will throw a light sediment. Should this occur allow the solid material to settle, carefully rack off the clear liquid into another demijohn, a small air space may be filled with a sugar syrup solution dissolved at the rate a quarter of a pound per pint (100g/ltr). If only a normal sediment forms leave the wine to stand at fermentation temperature for ten weeks and then rack in the normal way. A wine previously removed from the sediment and topped up with sugar syrup should be treated in the same way. After racking add 5ml of a stock solution of sodium metabisulphite or a campden tablet per gallon. It is important that apple wines are protected with sulphur dioxide at all stages as the liquid is readily oxidised and turns brown in colour.

GOOSEBERRY BASE

4lb (1.8kg) Gooseberries
1 litre White Grape Juice
2lb 6oz (1.1kg) Sugar
Pectic Enzyme
Yeast Starter

Gather the fruit when fully ripe, that is when the berries are soft to the touch but before they have turned an opaque colour (at which stage they are overripe). Crush the berries and place in the deep freeze for at least a week.

Day 1
Place the gooseberries together with any free run juice, the white grape juice and the dissolved sugar in the bucket. Make up to one gallon with tap water. Provide the pectic enzyme. Add 5ml of a stock solution of sodium metabisulphite or a crushed campden tablets. From now until fermentation is complete maintain at 18.5-21C (65-70F).

Day 2
Add the vigorously working yeast starter, stir the mixture daily.

Day 9
Strain, transfer to a demijohn, allow the liquid to ferment

to dryness in the usual way.

TO PRODUCE A FLOWERY BOUQUET IN ANY OF THE ABOVE WINES

Between days 2 and 6 of the fermentation, take two medium sized elderflower heads, remove the petals and place these in a piece of muslin or a jelly bag. The cloth or bag should be sewn up to stop the escape of the petals. Place the bag with the petals in a cup and scald with boiling water to destroy the wild yeasts. Allow to cool. Add both the water and the petals, still in the bag, to the fermentation bucket. Allow the bag to remain in the liquid for three days then remove it and discard the contents. This technique provides extra bouquet to any white wine. Alternatively you may prepare an elderflower wine (page 150) and blend to taste.

RHUBARB BASED

3lb (1.435kg) Rhubarb
1ltr carton White Grape Juice
2½lb(1.15kg) Sugar
Yeast Starter

Remove the leaves from the stalks and discard - these are poisonous. Remove the sheath at the base of the stalk, but do not peel or strip the outer skin from the stalk. Cut into pieces 2 inch (5cm) long. Store in the deep freeze for at least a fortnight. Transfer to the fermentation bucket and proceed as described above for Gooseberry Wine.

GRAPE BASED

Britain is at the northern extremity of the grape growing belt. The fruit can be cultivated in the South and Midlands and if you take care they can be used to make excellent dry white table wines. Due to their lack of body-producing materials they are far less successful when used for making other styles of wine. Unless you have an ideal site - such as against a south facing wall - it is likely that your grapes will be low in sugar and high in acid.

Ideally the wine should be made exclusively from grape juice. Obtain the juice by squeezing the berries in a wine press. If no wine press is available simply crush the berries with a potato masher in the fermentation bucket and ferment on the pulp. If the juice has an acidity between 4-8 ppt then you will not need to add water. With more acidic grapes measure the acidity and dilute accordingly aiming for an optimum acidity of 6 ppt.

The alternative approach is to add precipitated chalk. An addition of 7 grams of chalk reduces the acidity of 4.5 litres by 1.5 ppt (¼oz reduces a gallon by 1.5 ppt).

The other common problem with home produced grapes is that they contain insufficient sugar. Determine the gravity of the liquid and use the chart on page 76 to decide how much sugar to add.

Add 10ml of a stock solution of sodium metabisulphite or two campden tablets. Place in the fermentation temperature 18.5-21C (65-70F).

Day 2
Add the vigorously acting yeast starter. Stir daily.

Day 9
If the wine was fermented on the pulp, strain through

muslin and transfer to a demijohn. If the wine was made from free run juice decant the liquid from any heavy sediment and place in the demijohn. Top up and fit an airlock, finish as described for the wines above.

RED WINES FROM GRAPES

There are a small number of red grape varieties which will grow outdoors as well as the greenhouse variety Black Hamburg. These can be made into wine by exactly the same method as described for white grapes except that the fermentation must take place in the presence of the skins as even black grapes have colourless juice. Lightly crush the grapes. The extra tannin requires slightly more alcohol to balance it and the wine should be made from a starting gravity of 1.100.

Deep red wines of this type are ideal subjects for developing oakiness. This is achieved by adding 1 gram of oak chippings to the demijohn and storing the wine on it for at least two months.

ROSÉ WINES FROM GRAPES

Rosé wines can be made from red grapes by fermenting on the fruit for 3-5 days according to the intensity of colour that you wish to achieve. Acidity and sugar levels are checked and adjusted according to the method described for white table wines. The crushed fruit is added to the demijohn and, after treating with sulphur dioxide and standing overnight, the vigorously acting wine yeast is added. Watch the formation of the head and as soon as the whole of the surface is covered with a froth start counting the days. After 3-5 days strain the liquid into another fermenting bucket. After a total of 9 days from adding the yeast, strain the liquid and proceed as above.

Rosé wines are often drunk as medium sweet. They are best sweetened to taste using an artificial sweetener. You may sweeten with sugar and you will probably find a gravity of about 1.005-1.008 suitable. Immediately after providing extra sugar add a gram of potassium sorbate and one crushed campden tablet to stop refermentation.

Always store these wines in dark bottles away from direct sunlight.

DRY RED TABLE WINE

Red table wines need a robust taste capable of complimenting strongly flavoured dishes such as beef. The robustness and well developed character must not be confused with high astringency due to too much acid or tannin, which can be avoided by ensuring that there is not an excess of either component in the first place. This will also reduce the maturation period. Today the tendency is to make red wines which need only be kept for a relatively short period. Most table wines are ready for drinking about three months after clearing and the final racking. The two main bases for red dry wines are blackberry and elderberry.

Starting gravity 1.090
Final Gravity 1.000
Ideal Alcohol 13-14%
Acidity 5-7% ppt

BASIC ELDERBERRY WINE

2lb (900kg) Elderberries (weighed after removing from the stalks)
1½lb (700g) Raisins
2lb 6oz (1.1kg) sugar
2 x 5ml tsp Citric acid or acid mix
Pectic Enzyme
Yeast Starter.

Delay harvesting the fruit until the berries have had a deep red colouration for at least a week, but you must gather them before they begin to shrivel. If you delay too long there is a danger that the birds may beat you to it! Gathering dates vary, but the first week in October is usually a good time in most places, although in the South and in particularly warm coastal areas you will need to collect the fruit earlier than this.

Oxidation is less of a problem with elderberries than with many other fruits. Slight oxidation or caramelisation as a result of short time exposure to boiling water is usually lost amongst the strong flavours. The main task with elderberries is to separate the juice from the tannin rich skins. This is best done by using either a wine press or, if this is not available, a modified version of the hot water method.

Day 1
Remove the berries from the stalks, then weigh the fruits. Set aside half a pound (250g) of fruit, place the remainder in bucket and crush with a potato masher. Just cover with boiling water and allow to stand until cool enough to handle. Strain through a jelly bag into the fermenting bucket. Return the pulp to the original bucket, recover with boiling water and repeat the process, adding the liq-

uid from the second extraction to the first contained in the fermentation bucket. Using a press to perform the extraction the juice should be transfered to the bucket at this stage and from now onwards there is no difference in the procedures. Made from juice alone the wine loses much of its elderberry character. To overcome this problem, crush the remaining berries and add to the bucket. There will be sufficient skins to give the true elderberry flavour and the tannin will be at a reasonable level. Add the chopped raisins, make up to one gallon, then provide the pectic enzyme, and either 5ml of a stock solution of sodium metabisulphite or a crushed campden tablet. Cover and leave for one day. Maintain at the fermentation temperature of 18.5-21C (65-70F).

Day 2
Add the vigorously working yeast starter. Stir daily.

Day 9
Strain and transfer to a demijohn and finish in the usual way.

Such a drink prepared without any adjustments makes an excellent uncomplicated table wine, it can also be used as a base to be modified in a variety of ways to produce superior wines with a very vinous character similar to many commercial wines.

Three good variations use the base wine described above but with the elderberries reduced to 1½lb (700g) and the crushed fruit complete with their skins omitted.

Variation 1 Damsons
This gives a deep complex character to the wine, tending to disguise the predominance of the elderberries. Include with the base wine a pound and a half (700g) of damsons which should be cut but not stoned. This will increase the acidity and the added acid can be reduced to 5ml or adjusted after testing.

Variation 2 Loganberries
Loganberries are in season two months before elderberries but they can be stored in the deep freeze until required. Use the juice from the elderberries together with 2 pounds (900g) of loganberries and reduce the added acid to one 5ml.

Variation 3 Blackcurrants
Include with the pound and a half of elderberries a pound of blackcurrants and, as with damsons and loganberries, the added acid may be reduced to 5ml.

BASIC BLACKBERRY TABLE WINE
Blackberry is arguably the most versatile of all red winemaking ingredients, providing all of the necessary acid. Yet used on its own it tends to produce rather thin drinks. To make a quality red dry wine include 2lbs (900g) of sultanas (raisins tend to dominate with this particular fruit when making a dry wine).

3lb (1.35kg) Blackberries
2lb (900g) Sultanas
2¼lb (2.15kg) Sugar
Pectic Enzyme
Yeast Starter

Blackberries give a false impression of ripeness because they acquire a black colouration on the outside long before the acid has been replaced by sugars. At this stage the berries will be tart, and will not have developed the flavour. Delay gathering until the fruit is pleasantly sweet to taste. Select only sound berries. Avoid gathering the fruit after prolonged wet spells when they might be covered by mould spores which may have already started to cause decay and the mouldy taste that accompanies it.

Day 1
Remove any stalks and wash the fruit. If available, extract the juice using a wine press and transfer to the fermentation bucket. If you do not possess a press, place the fruit straight into the bucket and then crush it. Chop or mince the sultanas and add to the bucket, dissolve the sugar in water and add this. Make the volume up to a gallon. Provide the pectic enzyme and add 5ml of a stock solution of sodium metabisulphite or one crushed campden tablet. Cover the bucket and keep at the fermentation temperature of 18.5-21C (65-70F).

Day 2
Add the yeast starter, stir daily.

Day 9
Strain the juice into a demijohn, top up if necessary and finish the wine in the usual way.

Variation

BLACKBERRY AND BLACKCURRANT
3lb (1.35kg) Blackberries

½lb (250g) Blackcurrants
½lb (250g) Sultanas
2lb 10oz (1.2kg) Sugar
Pectic Enzyme
Yeast Starter

Blackcurrants used in small amounts will impart their own distinctive character on a wine. The crushed blackcurrant should be placed in the fermentation bucket together with the blackberries. Proceed according to the method described above.

ELDERBERRY AND BLACKBERRY DRY

2lb (900g) Blackberries
¾lb (350g) Elderberries
1lb (450g) Sultanas
2½lb (1.15kg) Sugar
1 x 5ml tsp of citric acid or acid mixture
Pectic Enzyme

Day 1
Place the elderberries and blackberries in the bucket and squash to break the skins, add the chopped sultanas and other ingredients and proceed according to the method given above.

ROSÉ

Rosé wines are intermediate between red and white wines, they are slightly more astringent than the latter and may be served with virtually any dish, although they are perhaps best suited to white meats such as pork. Many homemade rosés are prepared on the blending table, usu-

121

ally two or three measures of white wine to one of red. The mistake so often made with this wine is the belief that only the colour is mid way between the two main classes of wine. In fact it is mid way between the two in all respects. A small number of ingredients do lend themselves to making this style of wine.

Rosés are usually drunk as medium sweet wines

Starting Gravity 1.090
Final Gravity 1.005
Alcohol 12-13%
Acidity 6 ppt

RED CURRANT WINE

3lb (1.35kg) Red Currants
1ltr White Grape Juice
2lb 6oz (1.1kg) Sugar
Pectic Enzyme
Yeast Starter

Day 1
Crush the fruit and place in the fermentation bucket. Add the grape juice and the sugar dissolved to form a syrup. Make up to one gallon. Add 5ml of a stock solution of sodium metabisulphite or one crushed campden tablet and the pectic enzyme. Cover and leave for twenty four hours.

Day 2
Add the vigorously acting yeast starter and stir daily.

Day 9
Strain and transfer to a brown demijohn. If one is not available cover the glass with paper to omit light. Fer-

ment to dryness, add artificial sweetener and a campden tablet to protect the delicate colour. Alternatively you may add sugar syrup to taste. A reading of 1.005-1.007 on an hydrometer will provide the correct degree of sweetness. Then add a gram of potassium sorbate and a crushed campden tablet which will stop the recommencement of fermentation. Allow a month for the sweetener and any treatment to thoroughly mix then place in brown bottles.

Variation
The grape juice may be replaced with a pound of sultanas.

RASPBERRY WINE
Raspberries have a strong flavour which, when used in large amounts, tends to be overpowering. They make far better wines when the fruits are diluted with other fruits or juices.

Pick the fruit when soft yet still firm to the touch.

RASPBERRY AND APPLE WINE
2lb (900g) Raspberries
1ltr Apple Juice
1lb (450g) Sultanas
2½lb (1.15kg) Sugar
1 x 5ml tsp Citric acid or acid mix
Pectic Enzyme
Yeast Starter

Day 1
Squash the raspberries and place in the fermentation bucket together with the apple juice, the chopped sultanas and

the extra acid. Make up to a gallon (4.5ltr) with water.
Add 5ml of a stock solution of sodium metabisulphite.

Day 2
Add the vigorously acting yeast starter. Stir daily.
Finish the wine as described for Red Currant Wine above.

RASPBERRY AND RHUBARB WINE
Rhubarb is an excellent wine base or blending ingredient
for use with other fruit.

1½lb (700g) Raspberries
3lb (1.35kg) Rhubarb
2lb 10oz (1.25kg) Sugar
Yeast Starter

(Pectic Enzyme may be safely omitted from this recipe)

Day 1
Squash the raspberries and place in the bucket. Cut the
rhubarb stem below the bottom of the leaf and remove the
sheath attached to the base of the stem. Wash but do not
peel the rhubarb, cut into pieces about two inches in length
and add to the raspberries. Provide the sugar dissolved in
water and make up to one gallon (4.5ltr). Add 5ml of a
stock solution of sodium metabisulphite.

Day 2
Add the vigorously fermenting starter. Stir daily and finish as described for Red Currant Wine above.

DESSERT WINES
The home winemaker excels at making dessert wines. It

is possible to ferment drinks virtually as good as any you can buy. But just as they are expensive to purchase they will cost more to make and for the best results it is necessary to provide sufficient fruit. Some of the very best contain the equivalent of up to ten pounds of fruit per gallon.

Dessert wines should be high in all aspects of balance especially body, sweetness and alcohol; this in turn demands a higher acid level to overcome the buffer effect of the extra body and sweetness. Dessert wines can support a higher level of bouquet and flavour than most other drinks. Unlike lighter wines they are capable of carrying slight oxidation and caramelisation, and far from this being a fault it may add character and depth to the wine. It must be realised that oxidation is not always a fault. Many dessert wines do improve with age and an extended maturation is more beneficial than with most other types of wine, but it is also possible to enjoy a full fruit young dessert wine. The main difference in the production technique is associated with a need to produce the highest alcohol levels. This will necessitate the yeast working in optimum conditions and it is essential that a yeast nutrient is added. It is also necessary to feed the wine, by adding small additional quantities of sugar as the fermentation comes to its conclusion. This in turn will ensure the maximum conversion of sugar to alcohol, whereas if the sugar were all to be provided at the beginning, it could lead to difficulties in getting the fermentation to commence or may cause it to cease prematurely.

There are several different types of dessert wine and not all have the fullest body and highest alcohol.

White Dessert wines Initial Gravity 1.110
Final Gravity 1.010-1.015 (after addition of sugar following feeding)
Alcohol 16%+
Acidity 8-10 ppt

WHITE CURRANT

4lb (1.8kg) White Currants
2lb (900g) Sultanas
2lb 4oz (1kg) Sugar
Pectic Enzyme
Yeast Starter
Yeast Nutrient

Day 1
Remove the currants from the stalks, place in the bucket and crush. Add the chopped sultanas and the sugar dissolved to form a syrup. Make up to a gallon. Add 5ml of a stock solution of sodium metabisulphite or two crushed campden tablets. Provide the pectic enzyme, stand and maintain at the fermentation temperature of 18.5-21C (65-70F).

Day 2
Add the vigorously working yeast starter and the yeast nutrient. Stir daily.

Day 11
Strain and transfer the liquid to a demijohn. Fit an airlock.

Two Months After Starting The Wine
Rack the wine, check either by taste or with the hydrometer that it is dry. If it is not, return to the demijohn, top up with water and allow fermentation to proceed. If the

126

wine is dry add a further three ounces (75g) of sugar dissolved in sufficient water to top up the container and return to the fermentation temperature. Allow to ferment to dryness. Continue adding sugar and allowing to ferment to dryness until the wine remains sweet. If necessary add extra sugar to produce the desired level of sweetness.

The high sugar, acid and alcohol provide adequate protection from spoilage organisms. There is no need to add a campden tablet as the wine will be able to carry the oxidation which occurs on storage.

RHUBARB DESSERT WINE

4lb (1.8kg) Rhubarb
1lb (450g) Sultanas
2lb (900g) Bananas
½ pint (250ml) White or Yellow rose petals
2lb 10oz (1.2kg) Sugar
Pectic Enzyme
Yeast Starter
Yeast Nutrient

Week before Starting The Wine
Wash the stalks, cut into pieces two inches long without peeling and place in a container in the deep freeze.

Day 1
Place the pieces of rhubarb, the free run juice and the chopped sultanas in the fermentation bucket, together with peeled and mashed bananas. Add the sugar dissolved as a syrup and make up to one gallon. Add 5ml a stock solution of sodium metabisulphite or a crushed campden tablet. Provide the pectic enzyme. Cover and stand in the fermentation temperature 18.5-21C (65-70F).

127

Day 2
Add the yeast starter and yeast nutrient. Stir daily.

Day 7
Add the rose petals.

Day 11
Strain the juice into a demijohn, top up and fit an air lock.

Two Months After Starting The Wine
Rack and finish the wine as described for White Currant Wine.

PEACH DESSERT

4lb (1.8kg) Peaches
1ltr White Grape Juice
2¾lb (1.25kg) Sugar
1 tsp Citric acid or acid mix
Pectic Enzyme
Yeast Starter
Yeast Nutrient

Day 1
Prepare the fruit by removing the stones before placing in the fermentation bucket together with the white grape juice, the sugar dissolved as a syrup and the extra acid. Make up to one gallon with water. Add the pectic enzyme, 5ml of a stock solution of sodium metabisulphite or a crushed campden tablet. Cover the bucket and maintain at the fermentation temperature of 18.5-21C (65-70F).

Day 2
Provide the vigorously working yeast starter and the yeast nutrient. Stir daily.

Day 11
Strain the liquid, transfer to a demijohn, proceed and finish the wine according to the method described for White Currant Wine.

Variations
Apricot Wine - this is made by exactly the same method only the peaches are replaced by apricots.

PLUM WINE
Light coloured plums and even those with a red to purple skin will produce white wines or drinks with the lightest rosé tint which with keeping turns to gold.

5lb (2.25kg) Plums
1lb (450g) Bananas
1lb (450g) Sultanas
2lb 10oz (1.25kg) Sugar
1 x 5ml tsp Citric Acid or Acid Mix
Pectic Enzyme
Wine Yeast
Yeast Nutrient

Day 1
Prepare a 'banana gravy' by first discarding the skins and removing any traces of decay from the fruit. Place the bananas in a saucepan with a pint of water, bring to the boil and simmer for 30 minutes. Strain the juice through a jelly bag, giving a gentle squeeze. Place the liquid or

'gravy' in the fermentation bucket, discard the solid. It is not possible to remove the stones from plums, but the fruit should be cut to allow the liquid to come into contact with the flesh of the fruit. Add the sugar as a syrup and the acid. Make up to one gallon with water. Add 5ml of a stock solution of sodium metabisulphite or a crushed campden tablet followed by the pectic enzyme and place in the fermentation temperature 18.5-21C (65-70F).

Day 2
Add the vigorously acting yeast starter and the nutrient. Stir daily.

Day 11
Strain through a jelly bag, transfer to a demijohn, proceed and finish the wine by the method given for White Currant Wine.

Note that some plums have very red purple skins, certain varieties of cherry plums have red flesh and damsons, which are also much higher in acid and tannin, produce a red must. These should be used to make red dessert wines.

RED DESSERT WINES

Probably the best of all homemade wines, but for top quality dessert wines we are restricted to the same fruits that we used for table wines - blackberries and elderberries, with blackcurrants, loganberries and damsons employed to provide subtle variations.

Starting Gravity 1.100
Finishing Gravity 1.015-1.020 (after feeding and final sweetening)
Alcohol 16% +
Acidity 5-8 ppt

BLACKBERRY AND ELDERBERRY DESSERT

4lb (1.8kg) Blackberries
2lb (900g) Elderberries
1lb (450g) Raisins
2¾lb (1.25kg) Sugar
Pectic Enzyme
Yeast Starter
Yeast Nutrient

As with table wines it is important that the elderberries are separated from their skins which must be discarded. Because of the presence of the other fruit, which will provide the wine with depth of flavour, it is not necessary to include even a small percentage of the crushed berries.

Day 1
Prepare the elderberries by either squeezing the juice out with a wine press and adding the liquid to the blackberries or, alternatively, place the elderberries in another bucket or suitable large vessel, crush, cover with a pint of boiling water and allow to remain until cool enough to handle. Strain through a jelly bag into the bucket containing the blackberries. Perform a second extraction on the elderberries by returning the pulp to the original vessel, cover again with a pint of boiling water and repeat the process adding the extracted juice to the fermentation bucket. Make up to a gallon. Add the chopped raisins and the sugar dissolved as a syrup. Include 5ml of a stock solution of sodium metabisulphite or a crushed campden tablet. Provide the pectic enzyme, stand in the fermentation temperature of 18.5-21C (65-70F).

Day 2
Add the vigorously fermenting yeast starter together with the yeast nutrient. Stir daily.

Day 11
Strain the liquid, transfer to a demijohn and fit an airlock.

Six Weeks-Two months After Starting The Wine
Because of the large amount of fruit the wine may throw a very heavy sediment. If there is a thick layer of lees at the bottom of the container you should rack after six weeks. If not, you may delay for two months from the time that the wine was started, but no longer.

Rack the wine, note the taste. If there is any residual sweetness return to the demijohn, top up with water and ferment to dryness. When the wine is dry, either after initial racking or following refermentation add a further 3oz (75g) sugar dissolved in sufficient water to top up the demijohn. Repeat this feeding stage until the wine no longer referments. Adjust the sweetness to taste and bottle.

Variations
Subtle differences can be achieved by including another type of fresh fruit. Since this additional fruit will be present in relatively small amounts it is unlikely to have any marked effect on either the sugar present or the amount of acid. Include either 12oz (350g) of blackcurrants or 8oz (250g) of damsons in the recipe given above.

SWEET BLACKBERRY WINE
4lb (1.8kg) Blackberries
1lb (450g) Raisins

1½lb (700g) Bananas
2¾lb (1.25kg) Sugar
Pectic Enzyme
Yeast Starter
Yeast Nutrient

The wine is made by the method described above for Blackberry and Elderberry Dessert Wine, with the exception that the elderberries are omitted and a banana gravy is prepared by boiling the bananas with 1½ pints (800ml) of water and simmering for 30 minutes, the liquid is strained from the pulp and added to the fruit prior to topping up the bucket.

SWEET ELDERBERRY WINE

2lb (900g) Elderberries
1lb (450g) Bananas
1lb (450g) Raisins
2½ lb (1.15kg) Sugar
2 x 5ml tsp Citric Acid or Acid Mix
Pectic Enzyme
Yeast Starter
Yeast Nutrient.

Prepare the elderberries by squeezing in a wine press. Alternatively place the crushed berries in a bucket or large saucepan, add a pint of boiling water and allow to stand until cool enough to handle. Strain through a jelly bag into the fermentation bucket. Cover the pulp with boiling water and repeat the extraction, adding the juice to that from the first. Extract the bananas by first peeling and removing any signs of decay, and then bringing to the boil with a pint of water. Simmer for 30 minutes. Strain the juice into the fermentation bucket. Discard the pulp.

Add the chopped raisins, the extra acid and the sugar as a syrup. Make up to a gallon. Add the pectic enzyme and proceed as described for Blackberry and Elderberry Dessert Wine.

TAWNY DESSERT WINE

There are very few true examples of tawny commercial wines. Those which do occur are often the result of oxidation and maderisation taking place in the cask or bottle. This is a process which naturally takes many years to occur. There are, however, several ingredients which are themselves maderised as a result of the preservation process. Since the starting materials have already undergone oxidation there are no delicate flavours to protect. There is little point in using sulphur dioxide and the boiling water method of sterilisation, which is both quicker and more effective, may be employed in its place. Without the need to overcome the resistance of the sulphur dioxide, fermentation will be able to get under way quite effectively from a standing start and all that you need do is add a teaspoonful of the dried yeast. But include yeast nutrient to help obtain the higher alcohol level.

Specification as for red dessert wines.

ROSE HIP AND BANANA WINE

2lb (900g) Rose Hips
1½lb (750g) Bananas
½lb (225g) Dried Apricots
1lb (450g) Raisins
2½lb (1.15kg) Sugar
2 x 5ml tsp Citric Acid or Acid Mix
Pectic Enzyme

Traditional rose hip wines relied on gathering wild hips of the dog rose *(Rosa canina)*. This is a long and laborious process which can take several hours. Far larger and just as effective are the hips of garden roses. Make sure that the hips are fully ripe, ideally they should be gathered after the first frosts but before they have had the opportunity to turn black.

Day 1
Place the hips between two layers of cloth and crush with a rolling pin. Place in the bucket. Peel the bananas, remove any signs of decay then mash up and add to the bucket. Include the chopped raisins and apricots before adding three pints (1.25ltr) of boiling water. Allow to stand for ten minutes, add the sugar and stir to dissolve. Make the volume up to one gallon with tap water. Add the extra acid, pectic enzyme, and a teaspoonful of dried yeast together with the yeast nutrient. Place in the fermentation temperature, 18.5-21C (65-70F).

Day 10
Strain the liquid into the demijohn. Top up with water. Fit an airlock.

Six Weeks To Two Months After Starting The Wine
If a heavy sediment has formed after six weeks or bubbles have ceased to escape from the airlock, rack. Where bubbles still continue to escape from the airlock delay racking for a further fortnight but no longer. After racking check whether the wine is dry. If it is, then feed with

2 ounces (50g) of sugar, return to a demijohn and fit an airlock. Repeat this procedure until the wine remains sweet. Allow the wine to remain in the demijohn and clear. Bottle without treating with sulphur dioxide. Very much a wine for keeping it improves considerably with age.

Maturation Note. The addition of an oak flavour does not improve this particular wine, which derives much of its character from the caramelisation. This feature can be further developed, and the maturation process speeded up, by using two ounces of Demerara sugar in place of white household sugar at the first feeding.

SHERRY TYPE WINES

The distinctive flavour of sherry occurs as a result of a yeast flora, a film which forms over the surface of the wine in aerobic conditions. Whilst many yeasts will form films on the surface under aerobic conditions the uniqueness of this particular type is that it grows in wines of up to 16% alcohol. This is a far higher alcohol level than would support the majority of spoilage organisms which can grow in wine. Also the presence of the flor is extremely localised. Whilst from time to time amateur winemakers do claim to have developed a sherry flor on their wine, it is far more likely that they have a lower alcohol drink that has been infected with nothing more exciting than 'flowers of wine' which will soon destroy it.

The home winemaker must seek other ways of achieving the unique taste of sherry. This can be done by using ingredients which mimic the flavours you are trying to create, and by allowing the controlled atmospheric oxidation of high alcohol wines, which will not become infected under aerobic conditions. It must be realised that in the creation of a sherry style drink only a very limited and controlled amount of oxidation is required and it must be carefully monitored. Should you overexpose the wine to air it will be ruined. Oxidation of wine by the air is another complex process which can proceed in different ways according to the conditions. It is impossible to predict the length of time that the wine needs to be exposed to the air and it will be necessary to taste small quantities weekly to follow the progress of oxidation. As soon as it has oxidised sufficiently the process should be concluded by bottling the wine to exclude the air. Should you overoxidise a sherry you will probably be able to blend with another of the same type which has not been subjected to the oxidation process.

Since sherry production involves oxidation, sulphur dioxide performs no real purpose and the wine should be prepared by the hot water method.

DRY SHERRY TYPE

One of the few ingredients which is suitable for making a dry sherry are parsnips. The wine tends to be slightly thin in keeping with the style, which, together with a high alcohol level and relatively low acidity, yields the desired aperitif.

Starting Gravity 1.100
Finishing gravity 1.000
Alcohol 16% +
Acidity 4·5ppt

PARSNIP WINE (dry sherry type)

Parsnips should not be used for winemaking until after the frosts have had a chance to act on the roots. The older the roots the better the flavour. Traditionally this most popular of country wines was made from the last of the roots which were dug up in March before they started to reshoot.

3lb (1.35kg) Parsnips
1lb (450g) Mild Raisins
1ltr White Grape Juice
2lb 10oz (1.20kg) Sugar
1½ tsp Citric Acid or Acid Mix
Pectic Enzyme
Starch Enzyme (Amylase)
Wine Yeast
Yeast Nutrient

Day 1

Scrub the parsnips but do not peel, cut into pieces and place in a saucepan. Cover with 2 pints of water, bring to the boil and simmer for half an hour. Strain the liquid, whilst still hot, onto the chopped sultanas. Allow to cool. Dissolve the sugar in water, add the grape juice, syrup and acid to the other ingredients in the bucket. Make up to one gallon with water straight from the tap. Add the pectic and starch enzymes, the yeast and nutrient. Stand in the fermentation temperature of 18.5-21C (65-70F).

Day 8

Strain the liquid, transfer to a demijohn and ferment until bubbles cease to escape from the airlock. At this stage the wine should be dry. Although the aim is produce a high alcohol wine it should not be fed as it is not possible to know exactly how much sugar will ferment out and you could be left with a sweet wine. After racking top up with water and allow the wine to stand until it is clear. Divide the liquid equally into two demijohns, so that each is only half full. Plug the hole with cotton wool to stop the entry of dust. Stand in a cool room. After a month taste a small sample of the wine to determine whether it possesses the correct degree of oxidation. If it does not, allow to remain exposed to the air and regularly retest. Once the wine is sufficiently oxidised it may be bottled for drinking.

SWEET SHERRY TYPE

Using suitable ingredients it is not always necessary to subject the wine to atmospheric oxidation as it may already possess the desired characteristics.

Starting Gravity 1.100
Finishing Gravity 1.015 (after the addition of feeding or sweetening sugar)
Alcohol 16% +
Acidity 5ppt

PRUNE WINE

1½lb (700g) Prunes
1lb (450g) Raisins
2lb 6oz (1.05kg) Sugar
1½lb (700g) Bananas
2 x 5ml tsp Citric Acid
Pectic Enzyme
Wine Yeast
Yeast Starter
Yeast nutrient

Day 1

The prunes should be scored with a knife to aid their separation from the stones, the raisins chopped, and then placed in a bucket. Cover with three pints (1.5ltr) of boiling water. Extract the bananas by simmering with 1½ pints (750ml) of water for 20 minutes and straining the liquid into the bucket. Add the sugar as a syrup and make up to a gallon with tap water. Allow to reach the fermentation temperature 18.5-21C (65-70F).

Add the pectic enzyme, dried yeast and yeast nutrient. Stir daily, in the process attempting to separate the stones from the flesh of the prunes, wherever possible removing them from the bucket. On prolonged exposure the newly forming alcohol will leach substances from the stones which will give the wine a 'woody' flavour which is quite different from oakiness and which detracts from the wine. Providing that the fermentation is only allowed to proceed on the must for 7-10 days this should not be a serious problem, but to avoid the possibility of an off flavour it is always better to remove the stones of any member of the Prunus group before or during fermentation.

Day 8

Strain the liquid, transfer to a demijohn, make up the volume with tap water and fit an airlock.

When Bubbles Cease To Escape From The Airlock

Unless you check the level with an hydrometer, it is difficult to predict with this recipe how much sugar is present, due to the large amount of sugar-rich dried fruit. The quantity can vary quite considerably as will the time necessary to complete each stage. Delay racking until carbon dioxide ceases to be generated. Should this progress beyond two months from the time that you started the wine, rack. Feed the wine and continue to rack until you have a full bodied sweet wine. This should not require extra oxidation, but if it does use the method described for Parsnip Wine.

COUNTRY WINES

Country wines are made for the characteristic aroma and taste that the ingredient produces. In mature wine this may be very different from that of the fruit or vegetable from which it was made. Many country wines are curiosities, of little worth other than being of interest. Others are drinks worthy of consideration in their own right. Such wines with their variety of tastes extend the range of the cellar and every winemaker should aim to make at least some of them.

FRUIT WINES

Included in this category are those fruit wines which are not drunk with meals, but have sufficient taste and flavour to be enjoyed on their own.

The specification tends to be wider than with other types but falls within the following ranges:

Starting Gravity 1.090-1.100
Finishing gravity 1.005-1.015 (after sweetening if necessary)
Alcohol 13-15%
Acid level 4-8ppt

STRAWBERRY WINE

4lb (1.8kg) Strawberries
1ltr White Grape Juice
2½lb (1.15kg) Sugar
1 x 5ml tsp Citric Acid
Pectic Enzyme
Yeast Starter

Day 1

Gather the fruit after a dry spell, never following rain and avoid any which have the grey hairy growth of the fungus Botrytis. Place the fruit in the bucket and crush with a potato masher, do not attempt to puree by using a food processor. Add the grape juice, the acid, the sugar as a syrup and make up to one gallon. Provide 10ml of a stock solution of sodium metabisulphite or two crushed campden tablets. Allow to reach the fermentation temperature 18.5-21C (65-70F).

Day 2

Add the vigorously working yeast starter. Stir daily.

Day 8

Stain the liquid through a jelly bag, transfer to an airlock and ferment to dryness.

The wine should be drunk as medium to sweet, but should not be as sweet as a full dessert wine which tends to produce a cloying effect in this style of drink. Restrict the feeding to 2oz (50g) of sugar until such time as the wine is no longer dry. Make slight adjustments to taste. Aim for a final gravity of about 1.010. Strawberry is an extremely delicate wine which during the early stages of production may be a light pink colour which rapidly

142

changes to a brown, almost golden, hue. This colour together with the delicate flavour must be protected by the addition of 5ml of a stock solution of sodium metabisulphite or one crushed campden tablet per gallon. Bottle and drink the wine three months after clearing.

SLOE WINE

The secret of making sloe wine is to allow the fruit to remain on the bushes until late October, by which time the sharp acids will have given away to extra sugars and an almond like flavour will have developed in the fruit.

2lb (900g) Sloes
1lb (450g) Bananas
1lb (450g) Raisins
2½lb (1.15kg) Sugar
Pectic Enzyme
Yeast Starter

Store the bananas and the sloes in the deep freeze for at least a week before using.

Day 1

Transfer from the deep freeze to the fermentation bucket, add the chopped raisins and the sugar dissolved as a syrup. Make up to one gallon. Allow to reach the fermentation temperature 18.5-21C (65-70F), add the pectic enzyme and 5ml of a stock solution of sodium metabisulphite or two crushed campden tablets.

Day 2

Provide the vigorously acting yeast starter and stir daily.

Depending upon the ripeness of the fruit and the length of time in the deep freeze the round stones will start to separate cleanly from the flesh of the fruit and sink to the bottom of the container. Where this occurs remove as many of the stones as practical with a spoon.

Day 8
Strain the liquid from the solids. It is important with this wine that the fermenting liquid is not allowed to remain in contact with the fruit beyond this stage. The fruit undergoes natural decay, acquiring a brown colouration and the wine becomes plumy.

Ferment until gas bubbles no longer escape from the airlock. Rack. The wine should be sweet. Adjust to taste by the addition of sugar syrup. Gravity guide 1.007-1.010.

DAMSON WINE
A very useful ingredient which is often mixed with other fruits. It can be used on its own to make either a dry or social style wine. The dry wine is an especially useful stock wine for blending purposes.

3lb (1.35kg) Damsons
1ltr Red Grape Juice
2¾lb (1.25kg) Sugar
Pectic Enzyme
Wine Yeast

Once picked damsons quickly lose their essential freshness and the winemaker should aim to use the fruit the day that they are obtained. The skins are usually covered with wild yeasts, but the sulphur dioxide method is fully effective and does suppress the oxidation to which they are prone.

Day 1
Place the fruit, grape juice and the sugar dissolved as a syrup in the fermentation bucket. Make up to one gallon, provide the pectic enzyme and 10ml of a stock solution of sodium metabisuphite or two crushed campden tablets.

Day 2
Add the vigorously working yeast starter. Stir daily.

Day 8
Strain, gently squeezing the solids. Transfer to a demi-john. Fit an airlock and ferment to dryness.

The wine may either be drunk dry, when it should be protected by the addition of a crushed campden tablet per gallon, or sweetened to produce a social style wine with sugar or artificial sweetener added to taste. It should be stored for three months for the sugar to marry with the wine and then bottled and drunk.

MORELLO CHERRY WINE

3½lb (1.55kg) Morello Cherries
1ltr carton White Grape Juice
2lb 10oz (1.20kg) Sugar
Pectic Enzyme
Wine Yeast

Prepare as for damson wine.

DESSERT CHERRY WINE

4lb (1.8kg) Dessert or wild Cherries
1lb (450g) Sultanas
2½lb (1.15kg) Sugar
Pectic Enzyme
Wine Yeast

The wine is made by the method described for damsons with the grape juice replaced by chopped sultanas. Due to the pronounced flavour this wine can be drunk as a sweet social style. After fermentation is complete sweeten to taste, add a crushed campden tablet together with a gram of potassium sorbate per gallon. Store for three months, bottle and drink.

LOGANBERRY WINE

The same recipe and method is equally suitable to Tayberries.

3½lb (1.55kg) Loganberries
1ltr carton Red Grape Juice
2lb 10oz (1.2kg) Sugar
Pectic Enzyme
Wine Yeast

Gathering the fruit should be delayed until it has acquired a deep purple colouration. It should be soft but not at the stage where the slightest pressure results in a squashed berry. Do not gather following rain as the fruit may be infected by botrytis spores which may affect the taste.

Day 1
The juice may be extracted from the berries either by

using a wine press, or by employing a boiling water extraction described on page 131 for elderberries, both methods involve using only the juice. The wine can be made by fermenting on the pulp after leaving the fruit in the deep freeze for a week. Place the juice or pulp in the bucket together with the grape juice and the sugar dissolved as a syrup. Make up to a gallon with water. Add the pectic enzyme and protect with 5ml sodium metabisulphite, or a crushed campden tablet. Maintain at the fermentation temperature 18.5-21C (65-70F).

Day 2
Add the yeast starter and stir daily.

Day 8
If necessary strain, transfer to a demijohn, top up and ferment to dryness.

Rack and bottle when clear.

Loganberry wine is best served as a dry wine, it may be used as a table wine and is very useful for blending purposes.

RASPBERRY WINE
2lb (900g) Raspberries
1ltr carton of White Grape Juice
2¾lb (1.25kg) Sugar
Pectic Enzyme
Wine Yeast

Raspberries have too powerful a flavour for a dry wine and should be used either for a rosé or further sweetened to make a social style wine. The wine is made by the method described above for loganberries except that after racking the wine should be sweetened to taste with sugar, adding a campden tablet to protect the colour and a gram of potassium sorbate to stop refermentation. Allow the wine to mature for two months, bottle. It may be drunk immediately. As with most rosés it is not advisable to keep for longer than a year.

BANANA WINE

Bananas are mainly used as an adjunct to provide wines with body, but they can be used to make a very distinctive wine with the typical flavour of the fruit.

3lb (1.35kg) Bananas
1lb (450g) Sultanas
2½lb (1.15kg) Sugar
2½ tsp Citric Acid
Pectic Enzyme
Starch Enzyme (Amylase)
Wine Yeast

Use fruits which are overripe, remove the skins. If the bananas have any brown patches then this material can be included providing that it is not in an advanced stage of decay.

Place the bananas in a saucepan with two pints (1.2ltr) of water. Bring to the boil and simmer for 30 minutes. Strain the hot liquid onto the chopped raisins in the bucket. Add the sugar as a syrup, the acid and the pectic and starch enzymes. Make up to one gallon with tap water. When the temperature has reached 18.5-21C (65-70F) add the wine yeast.

Day 7 (do not delay this stage)
Strain the liquid and transfer to the demijohn. Allow to remain until bubbles cease to escape from the air lock. Rack.

After Racking
The wine should be medium to sweet and can carry the maximum alcohol level. If the wine is dry feed with 2 ounces (50g) of sugar and referment. The flavour, body and strength of this wine lends itself to maderisation. If you wish you may speed up the natural process by including 2 ounces (50g) of Demerara sugar at the initial fermentation stage and reducing the quantity of white sugar by a similar amount.

FLOWER WINES

Flowers provide only bouquet and flavour, but unlike many ingredients they change very little on keeping and consequently produce delicious wines that leave you with the sensation that you are actually drinking the flower itself.

Many flowers have been used for winemaking - dandelion, gorse, broom and primrose. These possess very little bouquet and although the drinks are often very good it is the base wine which is dominating and would almost certainly be just as acceptable had the flowers been omitted.

Two flowers which do make excellent wines are elderflowers and rose petals.

Either of these flowers used in the quantities given below can be incorporated in any of the dry white recipes given on page 110 or the sweet white wine recipes given on page 124.

DRY ELDERFLOWER WINE

Elderflowers are best suited to dry wines but can also be used for sweet wines. This recipe is for a dry wine.

6 Medium sized Elderflower Heads
1½lb (700g) Sultanas
2¼lb (1kg) Sugar
1½ x 5ml tsp Citric Acid
6 drops of grape tannin solution
Pectic Enzyme
Yeast Starter

Day 1
Place the chopped sultanas, the sugar dissolved as a syrup and the acid in the bucket. Make up to a gallon, add 5ml of a stock solution of sodium metabisulphite or a crushed campden tablet. Add the pectic enzyme and the tannin solution. Allow to stand at the fermentation temperature 18.5-21C (65-70F).

Day 3
Add the vigorously working yeast starter. Stir daily.

Day 4
Gather the elderflowers, smelling the blooms to ensure that they have a banana-like flavour. Make sure that they are free from insects. Remove the petals and place in a muslin bag weighted and attached to a piece of string.

Allow the bag to sink to the bottom of the bucket with the string draped across the top. The elderflower petals may be infected with wild yeasts, but these will be unable to compete with the vigorously fermenting wine yeast and in the anaerobic conditions that it forms will not be a problem.

Day 7
Remove the bag of petals, strain the liquid, transfer to a demijohn, and top up.

As soon as the mixture stops fermenting
Rack, add one crushed campden tablet, return to the demijohn, top up with water or grape juice. The wine will be ready for drinking three months after it has cleared.

SWEET ROSE PETAL WINE

Rose petals are only suitable for flavouring a sweet wine. The intensity of perfume will vary between the different varieties of rose and the vintner will need to experiment to ascertain the correct amount to use. The colour is also variable, white and yellow roses produce white wines whereas the deep red varieties tend to produce rosé colours as the newly formed alcohol leaches out the pigment.

1-2 pt (0.5-1.0ltr) (depending on intensity of perfume) Rose petals
1lb (450g) Sultanas
1lb (450g) Bananas
2 Medium Sized Oranges
2lb 10oz (1.25kg) Sugar
1 x 5ml tsp Citric Acid
Pectic Enzyme

Yeast Starter
Yeast Nutrient

Day 1
Prepare a 'banana gravy', peel the fruit, remove any signs of decay, bring to the boil with a pint of water and simmer for 30 minutes. Strain the liquid into the bucket discarding the pulp. Allow to cool. Add the sultanas, the juice of the oranges together with the sugar dissolved as a syrup. Make up to a gallon with tap water, add the pectic enzyme and 5ml of a stock solution of sodium metabisulphite or a crushed campden tablet.

Day 2
Add the vigorously working yeast starter. Stir daily.

Day 4
Add the rose petals. The part of the petals that provide the essential oils are the scent glands at the base. There is no need to use blooms in prime condition, wait until the flowers have blown, gather just the petals, place them in a large muslin bag or similar, weighted to make it sink, and drop it into the fermentation bucket. Since there is a relatively large amount of decaying plant material it should only be allowed to remain in contact for a maximum of three days. The essential oils will dissolve out in this time.

Day 7
Remove the bag of petals, allow the primary fermentation to continue until the vigorous stage subsides.

Day 9-11
Strain the liquid, transfer to a demijohn, top up and fit an

airlock.

When Bubbles Cease Escaping From The Airlock
Rack and, if the wine is dry, feed with 2oz portions of sugar until a sweet wine is obtained. When clear, bottle.

CEREAL WINES
Cereals impart a very strong flavour which is extracted mainly from the husks of the grain, it is complimented by oxidised caramelised flavourings.

1lb (450g) Crushed Wheat
1½lb (700g) Raisin (strong flavoured muscatels are best)
2¼lbs (1kg) White sugar
4oz Demerara Sugar
Juice of two oranges
2 x 5ml tsp Citric Acid
Pectic Enzyme
Starch Enzyme (Amylase)
Wine Yeast

Day 1
Chop the raisins, crush the cereal and place in the fermentation bucket together with the chopped raisins. Cover with three pints of boiling water. Add the sugar as a syrup. Make up to one gallon and allow to reach the fermentation temperature 18.5-21C (65-70F). Add the acid, pectic and starch enzyme and a teaspoonful of yeast. Stir daily.

Day 9
Strain the liquid, transfer to a demijohn, top up and fit an airlock.
    Finish the wine as described for white dessert wines.

Barley may be used in place of wheat when a very similar wine is obtained.

VEGETABLE WINES

Apart from parsnips (page 138) the only other vegetable which makes a quality wine is carrots. Carrot wine has a strong well developed flavour and is not suitable for blending with other drinks. It may be drunk socially or as an aperitif.

3lb (1.35kg) Carrots
1lb (450g) Raisins
2½lb (1.15kg) Sugar
2 x 5ml tsp Citric Acid
Pectic Enzyme
Starch Enzyme (Amylase)
Yeast

Day 1

Wash and chop, but do not peel the carrots. Bring to the boil with 3 pints of water and simmer for thirty minutes. Strain the liquid onto the chopped raisins, add the sugar dissolved as a syrup and make up to one gallon. Provide the pectic and starch enzymes and the yeast. Place in the fermentation temperature 18.5-21C (65-70F) and stir daily.

Day 8

Strain, transfer to a demijohn, top up and fit an airlock. Maintain at the fermentation temperature until bubbles cease to escape from the airlock. Rack. Carrot is drunk as a medium to medium sweet wine so adjust the gravity to 1.007-1.010. Add a crushed campden tablet to suppress refermentation.

CITRUS WINES

Citrus wines make excellent aperitifs.

Starting Gravity 1.100
Finishing gravity 1.000 (or less)
Alcohol 16% +
Acidity 7-10 ppt

SEVILLE ORANGE WINE

3lb (1.35kg) Seville Oranges
2½lb (1.15kg) Sugar
1ltr White Grape Juice
Pectic Enzyme
Yeast Starter

Day 1
It is only the juice which is required and any method of extracting may be employed. The fruit should be peeled, the segments separated and placed in a wine press or food processor. Pith will give any citrus wine a bitter taste and it is essential to ensure that all traces are omitted from the must. Place the liquid, the chopped or minced sultanas and the sugar dissolved as a syrup in the fermentation bucket. Make up to one gallon with tap water and provide the pectic enzyme. Add 5ml of a stock solution of sodium metabisulphite or a crushed campden tablet.

Day 2
Add the vigorously acting yeast starter, stir daily.

Day 9
Strain, place in a demijohn, fit an airlock and ferment to

155

dryness.

Rack when fermentation is complete. Add one crushed campden tablet per gallon and bottle after three months.

GRAPE FRUIT WINE

2ltr carton Grape Fruit Juice
2ltr carton White Grape Juice
2lb (900g) sugar
6 drops Grape Tannin Solution
Pectic Enzyme
Yeast Starter

Day 1

Place the grape fruit juice, the grape juice, the sugar made up as a syrup, and the grape tannin in the fermentation bucket. Make up to one gallon, add 5ml of stock solution of sodium metabisulphite or a campden tablet. Maintain at the fermentation temperature 18.5-21C (65-70F).

Day 2

Add the vigorously working yeast starter. Stir daily.

Day 8

Transfer the liquid to a demijohn, fit an airlock and ferment to dryness.

Rack when bubbles are no longer seen to be escaping from the airlock. Allow to stand until clear, reracking if necessary.

The wine is drunk as a dry aperitif.

ORANGE WINE

This should be made as a relatively high alcohol wine

with the residual sugar syrup providing extra body. Can be drunk at the end of a meal as a liqueur.

Starting Gravity 1.100
Finishing Gravity 1.013 (with added sweetening sugar)
Alcohol 16% +
Acidity 6-8 ppt

2ltr carton Orange Juice
1ltr carton White Grape Juice
2½lb (1.15kg) Sugar
6 drops of Grape Tannin
Pectic Enzyme
Wine Yeast

Prepare as described for Grape Fruit Wine but feed to produce a maximum alcohol sweet dessert wine.

When the wine has fermented to dryness it should be racked and the volume made up with two ounces (50g) sugar dissolved in sufficient water to fill the space. Continue racking and feeding until a sweet wine remains. Gravity should be 1.010-1.015.

OTHER FRUIT JUICE WINES

Fruit juices on sale at the supermarket are an excellent source of ingredients for making wine and avoid the necessity to extract the liquid. The quality of the drink which the juice produces will vary with the particular type of fruit, but many hold the potential to yield very worthwhile wines. Because of the diversity of these products the wine maker will need to carry out some experiments with the less familiar juices, checking the acid level and adjusting accordingly. When a suitable must has been compounded the wine can be made by using the method described for Orange Wine (page 157) and replacing the orange juice with 2 litres of the chosen fruit juice.

VERMOUTH STYLE WINE.

Vermouth is a distinctive style of aperitif, relying upon its high alcohol content, high acidity and the bitter palate cleansing character of the herbs, particularly wormwood. A good homemade Vermouth style wine requires a suitable base wine together with a successful extraction of the correct herb mixture.

Starting Gravity 1.100
Finishing gravity 1.000 (or lower)
Alcohol 15-16%
Acidity 8-10 ppt

1 can White Grape Juice Concentrate
1ltr Carton of Grape fruit Juice
12oz (350g) Sugar
1 Pkt Vermouth Herbs
Wine Yeast
Yeast Nutrient

All the ingredients should be sterile, and any oxidation will be concealed by the strong flavour of the herbs, so it is unnecessary to use sulphur dioxide. Similarly there is no need to include pectic enzyme.

Prepare the wine as described for grape juice concentrate, page 94. Do not add the herbs until the wine has cleared. Place the herbs in a muslin bag and insert in the demijohn. The average extraction period is a fortnight. However, after a week you are advised to make daily tastings and remove the herbs when you judge the taste to be right. Once flavoured the wine may be drunk immediately. Being a high alcohol, high acid wine it will keep for several months.

Dry Rhubarb wine (page 113) is an excellent alternative base wine, the subtle flavour of the rhubarb itself bestowing a piquancy to the aperitif. To produce a high alcohol level, so important with this style of wine, increase the amount of sugar to 2lb 12 ounce per gallon (1.3kg/4.5ltr). The overall quality of the wine can be improved by the addition of vodka to taste.

SWEET VERMOUTH

Described as a sweet aperitif it is the astringency of the herbs which makes this a suitable wine for drinking before meals.

Starting Gravity 1.100
Finish gravity 1.010 (after sweetening)
Alcohol 15-16%
Acidity 6-8 ppt

As with the dry version any dessert base is suitable for converting into a sweet vermouth style, but again rhubarb is arguably the most suitable. Prepare the base wine as described for Rhubarb Dessert Wine (page 127), feed to increase the alcohol and sweeten. Extract the herbs in a similar manner as described for the dry version.

GINGER WINE

The addition of ginger to a wine to conceal its faults was

recognised at an early stage in the development of country wines and many traditional recipes exist which in reality are little more than ginger wines although often of a very low quality. The true ginger wine is a sweet raisin wine to which ginger is added. The strong flavours coupled with the high alcohol content allow the use of the quicker boiling water method. The method of extraction of the flavouring differs from that described for Vermouth in that it is more effective when performed in the fermentation bucket.

¾oz (20g) Root Ginger
1½lb (700g) Raisins
2½lb (1kg) Sugar
2 tsp Citric Acid
Pectic Enzyme
Wine Yeast
Yeast Nutrient

Day 1
Bruise the ginger, chop the raisins and place in the bucket. Cover with four pints of boiling water. Add the sugar and stir until dissolved, then provide the acid. Make up to one gallon with tap water, add the pectic enzyme and the yeast.

Day 8
Strain the liquid into the demijohn, top up if necessary, fit an airlock and ferment until bubbles cease to escape. Rack. If the wine is still dry, feed with 2oz (50g) portions of sugar until sweet. The final gravity should be 1.050-1.015 depending upon the preferred level of sweetness. The wine may be drunk as soon as it is clear. This is a wine which can carry maderisation. If you like this characteristic you

may replace 2-4 ounces (50-100g) of the white sugar, added prior to the commencement of fermentation, with an equal quantity of Demerara sugar.

SPARKLING WINES

Sparkling wines differ from other types in that much of their character depends upon the dissolved carbon dioxide which they contain and the effervescence when the liquid is released from the bottle. The quality of the wine will depend upon both the quantity of the carbon dioxide and the wines ability to slowly release the gas. The latter is reliant upon the retentive qualities of the liquid and the gradual rise in temperature as the wine, which was poured cold, gradually rises to atmospheric temperature in the glass. Due to the need to recommence fermentation in the bottle, making the yeast start working again in what is to it an increasingly hostile environment, the wines are made of lower alcohol level than in other cases. This demands extra vigilance as far as hygiene is concerned.

The Basic Technique

A relatively low alcohol level wine is prepared using the same general method as is employed to make white table wines. As soon as the wine appears to have finished fermenting check that it is dry, the hydrometer reading should be below 1.000 and there should be no discernable sweetness on the palate. Do not proceed until the wine is completely dry, any residual sugar will ferment in the bottle in addition to that which you add later and could cause the bottle to explode. But once the wine is dry do not delay, such weak wines are very vulnerable to attack by spoilage organisms. Check that the wine is clear, where

161

necessary use finings, do not rely on a cloudy wine clearing in the bottle, it probably will not.

Choice of Bottles
It is essential that you employ Champagne or other bottles used for in-bottle fermentation. These are extra thick, capable of withstanding the considerable pressures that develop during this method of preparation. There are several sparkling wines on the market which are produced by injecting carbon dioxide into still wines. This process can be controlled within very strict pressure limits and consequently cheaper, thinner bottles can be used. They are suitable for the purpose for which they were designed, but can burst and are very dangerous if used for in-bottle fermentation. As the temperature rises dissolved carbon dioxide is expelled from the wine and the pressure builds up. This gas pressure is at its greatest when the wine is at fermentation temperature. Once fermentation is complete, whenever the wine is to be handled it should be allowed to stand in the refrigerator for two hours to reduce the pressure in the vessel. When opening sparkling wines always wrap a cloth around the bottle, this will not only provide limited protection to your hands should an accident happen, but insulates the bottle from the warmth of your hands. Always handle pressurised wine bottles with extreme caution.

SPARKLING GOOSEBERRY WINE
2½lb (1.15kg) Gooseberries
1ltr carton Grape Juice
2lb (900g) Sugar
¾tsp Citric Acid or Acid Mix

Place the gooseberries in the deep freeze for a week to break down the fruit.

Day 1
Place the gooseberries, the grape juice, the sugar dissolved as a syrup and the acid in the fermentation bucket. Make up to a gallon with tap water. Provide the pectic enzyme and 5ml of a stock solution of sodium metabisulphite or a crushed campden tablet.

This is the only stage in the production of a sparkling wine that sulphur dioxide is included - later additions will arrest the in-bottle fermentation so essential to this style of drink.

Day 2
Provide the vigorously working yeast starter and stir daily. The must is low in sugar and all stages of the fermentation process will be completed earlier than for other wines. Watch the surface of the liquid for the reduction in activity, as soon as the head subsides the liquid should be strained and transfered to a demijohn to further reduce the chances of infection. Expect to notice this from days 5-7 - the exact time will depend on several variables such as the temperature and the strain of the yeast.

In the Demijohn
Watch for the stage when bubbles stop escaping from the demijohn. Check that the wine is dry by tasting, if in doubt use the hydrometer. The gravity should be 0.099 or less. If the wine is still sweet - which is only likely to

occur if the liquid has been kept in conditions which are too cold - allow it to remain in the demijohn.

Rack, transfer temporarily to a demijohn, add finings if necessary. As soon as the wine has cleared bottle.

Bottling

Check six Champagne or similar bottles to ensure that they do not have any cracks or flaws, place in each the equivalent of a level teaspoonful of sugar dissolved in the minimum amount of water, artificial sweetener, (if a sweet wine is required) and two tablespoonfuls of a solution containing a vigorously acting yeast starter. Fill to within an inch of the top of the bottle with wine. Wire down the cork.

After Bottling

Return the bottles to the fermentation temperature 18.5-21C (65-70F) and stand there for three months.

Degorging

You may keep the wine for up to a year on the small amount of sediment. If you intend storing the wine for longer periods it will be necessary to remove the sediment. At anytime between six months and a year after bottling the wine, the sediment should be removed. This is done by turning the bottle upside down and standing in the refrigerator. This allows the sediment to settle in the neck of the bottle. Place the neck of the bottle in a container of ice to which approximately ten percent salt has been added. Allow to stand in the refrigerator to keep the body of the wine cool until a small solid plug has formed in the neck of the bottle. Wrap a cloth around the bottle and hold at an angle of 45 degrees. Using pliers, cut the wire and release the cork. Allow the pressure within the bottle to force the plug out. Immediately top up with cooled grape juice or water to an inch below the level where the cork will rest. Wire down the cork. The wine may be stored at normal temperatures until required.

Serving Sparkling Wines
For the dissolved gas to have full effect it is essential that the wine is served cold. This also reduces any dangers which may result from opening the pressurised bottles. Best results are obtained if the liquid is allowed to stand in the refrigerator for two hours before serving.

Variations

SPARKLING RHUBARB WINE
3lb (1.4kg) Rhubarb
1 carton White Grape Juice
2lb (900g) Sugar
Pectic Enzyme
Yeast Starter

Clean the rhubarb, use only the stalks, removing the leaves. Cut into pieces two inches long. Stand in the deep freeze for a week and make the wine as described above for Sparkling Gooseberry Wine.

SPARKLING APPLE WINE
Good sparkling wines can be made from apples providing that you have a blend which will clear. Any apple light dry table wine recipe can be adopted by reducing the added

sugar to 1lb 14oz per gallon (850g/4.5ltr). Alternatively because of the difficulty of extracting the juice from the apples you may use the following method:

2 x 1ltr carton Apple Juice
1ltr carton White Grape Juice
1lb 14oz (850g) Sugar
6 drops grape tannin solution
Pectic Enzyme
Wine Yeast.

Adopt the method described for Gooseberry Wine.

SPARKLING WINE FROM CONCENTRATES

1 can Light White Table Wine Concentrate
1 Carton White Grape Juice
8oz (225g) Sugar
Yeast Starter

All the ingredients will be sterile, the oxidation rate of grape juice is slower than that of apples and using this recipe it is not essential to treat with sulphur at all, providing that you initially add a vigorously acting yeast starter. In all other respects the wine should be made according to the method given for Sparkling Gooseberry Wine.

PINK SPARKLING WINES

Sparkling wines with a slight pink tinge are very popular, this effect can easily be created in any of the above recipes by adding the free flow liquid and pulp obtained from standing half a pound (225g) of either raspberries or red currants in the deep freeze for a week.

A similar effect can be achieved by replacing the white grape juice with red.

Flower Character

The presence of a flowery bouquet and flavour can add a great deal to sparkling wines. The only flower which is suitable for inclusion is elderflower. Use between three and six medium sized heads, which, when smelt, have a bouquet slightly reminiscent of bananas. The flowers will probably have wild yeasts and spoilage organisms on the surface. Normally the action of the yeast and the inbuilt protection of the wine itself are sufficient to overcome any problems, but with the lower alcohol sparkling wines, and the necessity to remove all traces of microbes, instant treatment is necessary. Remove the petals from the stalks and place in a cup, scald with boiling water and allow to cool. Add the petals and the sterilising water to the must. As the initial fermentation stage is shorter even than for table wines it is safe to allow the petals to remain in the liquid throughout this period and strain them out prior to transferring into the demijohn.

You may include elderflowers in any sparkling wine, white or pink, sweet or dry.

Sparkling wines are an often neglected aspect of our craft, but the rewards that they offer are amongst the greatest. It is possible to make good quality sparkling wines at home. The recipes given are amongst the best, but there are others, and using the principles explained, you can adjust recipes and make your own special type. And remember home made sparkling wines can be used to prepare Buck's Fizz and all of the other cocktails that are made from the equivalent bought wines.

LIQUEUR WINES

One of the latest products to appear on the homebrew market are liqueur type drinks which are made without the need to add expensive spirits. These are prepared by taking the alcohol level achievable by fermentation to the upper limit and adding a specially prepared flavouring.

It is doubtful if the average home winemaker will be able to consistently achieve alcohol level higher than the upper teens, but this is strong enough to produce very good liqueur type drinks.

These levels which may be considered as the highest attainable by fermentation are achieved by using a good strain of yeast and providing a perfectly balanced food in the form of yeast nutrient. The process is comparable with growing monster vegetables, you will only get the best results if you feed them properly. The slight differences in alcohol levels of the various brands probably depends more on the effectiveness of the nutrient than any other factor. If the yeast is to give of its best and survive longer in what to it is an increasingly hostile environment it must be allowed to grow without any stress. This can be achieved in part by maintaining a steady temperature, 21C (70F) or other recommended value. Any significant fluctuations may mean the yeast going dormant and needing to restart again, something which becomes increasingly difficult as the environment becomes more hostile. When making this type of wine if you are to get the best results it is essential that you follow the manufacturer's instructions exactly.

7: THE FINISHED WINE

BLENDING

We use science to explain the processes which occur during winemaking, but the winemaker is an artist. Having learnt the relatively easy skills of converting sugar into alcohol, the real quality of a drink depends upon the palate of its creator and his ability to adjust the drink to make that special brew. Good recipes, well made, will always provide you with sound wines, but they can always be improved. The perfect recipes have not been discovered, and they never will be, because they depend upon one person's idea of what is the ideal wine. By adjusting the standard recipes what you can seek to achieve is your own ideal wine.

Winemakers are sometimes reluctant to blend, but it can result in major improvements to the quality of the drinks and is a skill which is easily learnt. Remember no one is born with an educated palate, it is something which you need to acquire. But we all have a sense of taste and all we need do is to train it. And it is not difficult, most people can achieve it with just the minimum of totally enjoyable effort.

At its simplest blending is used to iron out faults, such

as too little or too much acid, simply by mixing a wine which is low in the characteristic with another which is high. This results in two gallons of wine both superior to either of the component gallons. This is an idealised case. You seldom have a gallon of wine whose faults are equal and opposite to that of another gallon, and if you used the procedures outlined in this book, you certainly will not have several wines over or under sweet, too acidic or lacking acid, or suffering from some obvious excesses or deficiencies. Although they may vary slightly from your ideal for the reasons previously discussed. Major deviations are the results of bad recipes, poor winemaking or a combination of the two. Blending should not be thought of as a method of correcting faults, but rather a fine tuning which produces the very best wines possible. Superb wines are complex, the intermingling of several different taste sensations. The importance of blending has long been appreciated in the commercial field with several well known wines being produced by the mixing of wines originating from different grape varieties, or even from different districts.

The recipes given in this book are, in the main, simple mixtures. They rely on just a few ingredients, but as you bring more tastes together you alter the nature of the wine usually for the better, and this can only be done initially on the blending table. Based on the amounts used you can modify your recipes accordingly in future years.

Where wines are being mixed together, if one is infected in any way the disease will spread to, and destroy, all of the wine involved in the blend. Only sound wines should be used for blending, it is not a method for curing diseased wines.

The Basic Technique

For the initial exercise in wine blending take four wine glasses and fill them with the relative amounts of each of the wines given in the table below.

	Glass 1	Glass 2	Glass 3	Glass 4
Wine A	100%	50%	25%	0%
Wine B	0%	50%	75%	100%

Taste the wine in glass 1 and then the three others in turn. Some people prefer to wash their mouth out with water between each tasting, but with a very small number of extremely similar wines you may find it better to allow tastes to linger. Whenever you assess widely differing wines, where there is a possibility of major faults, you should always wash your mouth out between tastings, but remember these are tips to help you and not hard and fast rules. What you are seeking to do when you blend is to make an improvement. When you have identified the improvement on a small scale you will need to know the relative proportions of each wine so that you will be able to achieve the same result in bulk.

Having determined which wine is the best, blend the larger quantities that are available. It will become clear that whilst this method gives one gallon of superb wine, you now have the choice to bottle the remainder as straight wines, in which case you still possess the same quantity as you had prior to the commencement of blending, or you further experiment to produce a second improved blend, although it is unlikely to be as good as your first choice.

This technique can be used to introduce a desirable characteristic into a wine such as floweriness into a table wine.

Let us assume that wine A is a sound, but slightly lacking in interest, table wine and that B is a straight elderflower. Blending both together you will either end up with a) a fifty-fifty mix or b) 75% table wine 25% elderflower - an improved table wine plus an equal amount of c) 75% elderflower and 25% table wine - an elderflower with a weakened bouquet which may be an improvement if the original was too strong, or an acceptable dilution if this were not the case. This approach to blending is simplistic, involving only two wines and the same number of basic styles. With practise you will be able to blend together more than two wines, including no more than hints of particular characteristics. As your knowledge of wine grows, so will your confidence and the ability to produce even better wines. Occasionally blending may result in the resultant wine becoming slightly hazy. This is caused by change in the tannin balance forming further precipitation. On standing the wine will soon throw a sediment and become clear once again.

Recipe Development

Blending is not an end, it is just a beginning. When you have produced the ideal wine from the composition of the blend you can now calculate the amounts of all the original ingredients which went into producing the particular finished blend. Armed with this information you should recalculate the recipe and use this as a basis to make next year's wine. If necessary, you can fine tune the following year until such time as you can make your ideal wine consistently without recourse to blending. It is this method, based on a scientific and mathematical approach to recipe formulation, that leads to the very best wines - often uniquely designer brewed to the winemaker's own palate and something he can never hope to buy.

ADJUSTING WINES

Sometimes it is possible to detect a deficiency - insufficient acid, sugar or tannin - in a wine and rather than blend, the shortfall can be made up by simple addition. Provide all additives as a solution at this stage. When sugar syrup is added it can take many days for the new liquid to marry with the old. If you hold a bottle of recently sweetened wine up to the light you will be able to detect the separate layers of the wine and syrup - a condition known as inhomogeneity. The effect disappears with time.

There is always a danger that a sweetened wine will referment.

THE SOLERA SYSTEM

This is a means used by commercial winemakers for ensuring that the character and quality of sherry remains the same over very many years. It has since been extended to other types of wine. The full commercial solera tends to be quite complicated, but consists basically of a system of interlinked barrels each containing wine of different ages. The oldest wine being in the barrel situated at the bottom, with other containers of progressively younger wine interlinked through a gravity feed system. A limited amount of wine is drawn off from the bottom barrel and at the same time an equal volume of new wine is placed in the uppermost barrel to keep the system topped up. When young wine of a very similar type and style is added to an old vintage it gradually takes on the character of the mature wine with the result that the wine withdrawn never alters from year to year.

Although it is not practical to make a multibarrel system, or to wait several years, it is possible to develop your own modified system base on the principles of a solera. The method is only suitable for high alcohol wines which have sufficient inbuilt protection to keep indefinitely and, before you embark on such a system, you will need to be sure that you have a recipe which you like and for which you are capable of obtaining the ingredients to make in future years. For this system you will need a nine gallon wooden barrel. Unless the barrel is new allow a stock solution of sodium metabisulphite to stand in the barrel for forty eight hours. Empty and rinse out.

Fill the barrel with the high alcohol wine the character of which you wish to perpetuate.

After one year draw off between a fifth and a third of the wine and fill the barrel with an equal amount of a wine made up to the same recipe as the original. Repeat the same procedure in future years. The method does differ from the solera system in one important respect - all wine both the youngest and the oldest are allowed to mix together. But once the system has been set up it has the advantage that when you have a clear wine which has finished fermenting you can use it to draw off an equal amount of instant aged wine from the system. It is particularly useful with rich dessert wines.

GLOSSARY OF TECHNICAL TERMS

ACETALDEHYDE
The first oxidation product of alcohol, responsible for much of the character of sherries.
ACETIC ACID
The harsh acid found in vinegar, detected as a burning sensation at the back of the throat.
AEROBIC FERMENTATION
Fermentation conducted in the presence of air.
ALCOHOL
A class of organic compounds, in winemaking usually taken to mean ethanol (ethyl alcohol).
AMYLASE
An enzyme which splits starch molecules down to glucose.
ANAEROBIC FERMENTATION
Fermentation conducted in the absence of air.
APERITIF
A wine drunk before a meal to stimulate the appetite.
AUTOLYSIS
The natural break down of the lees by its own enzymes of decay, resulting in a musty or composty taste.
BALANCE
The relationship between the various components of the

wine.

BLAND

Used to describe an insipid wine which lacks acid, tannin, alcohol or all three.

BODY

The thickness of a wine, its weight in the mouth.

BOUQUET

The aroma of the wine.

BRILLANT

Describes the highest degree of clarity of a wine.

CAMPDEN TABLET

Sodium metabisulphite made up in tablet form, used for sterilising equipment and ingredients and for stabilising wines.

CARBON DIOXIDE (CO2)

A gas consisting of one part carbon and two parts oxygen released during fermentation.

CITRIC ACID

Acid found mainly in citrus fruits and considered essential to fermentation.

CLARITY

The absence or presence of suspended solids.

CLOUDINESS

Suspension of insoluble particles in the liquid.

DECANTING

Pouring clear wine from its sediment formed during maturation.

DEMIJOHN

Fermenting vessel.

DESSERT WINE

The fullest and sweetest of all wines.

DRY

A wine which does not contain any discernable sugar.

ENZYMES
Biologically produced compounds that bring about chemical reactions.

FARWELL
The taste remaining in the mouth after drinking a wine.

FILTRATION
Physical separation of suspended particles to aid clarification.

FINING
Treatment of a wine to form giant molecules which will trap and precipitate suspend particles.

FLOR
Growth which may occur on sherry and produce the characteristic taste.

FORTIFICATION
The addition of spirit to increase the strength of wine.

FRUCTOSE
Sugar found in most fruit, produced from sucrose by inversion.

GERANIUM
Off flavour similar to that of a geranium, formed as a result of treating a wine with potassium sorbate without the addition of a campden tablet.

GLUCOSE
Sugar obtained together with fructose from sucrose by the process of inversion.

GLYCERINE
Compound responsible for much of the natural body of a wine. Can be added artificially in small quantities.

GOLDEN
A colour of wine, often develops as a result of aging. Where appropriate golden wines should be exhibited in white wine classes.

GREEN
Used to describe young wine which possesses a sharp taste due to its immaturity.

HARSH
A wine containing too much acid or tannin.

HAZE
The presence of minute suspended particles, usually due to starch or pectin, that cannot be removed by filtering.

INHOMOGENEITY
The appearance of distinct layers in a wine, the result of liquids of different density having not mixed. The effect is most noticeable when a wine is sweetened with sugar syrup, it disappears with time.

INITIAL FERMENTATION
The aerobic or logarithmic stage during which the yeast grows.

INVERSION
The enzymic breakdown of sucrose into glucose and fructose. The first stage in the conversion of sugar to alcohol.

LAG PHASE
The stage after yeast has been added to the must and before there is any discernable activity.

LEES
Sediment of dead yeast and fruit cells formed during fermentation.

LOGARITHMIC PHASE
The initial rapid fermentation when the yeast cells are growing rapidly to occupy the space available.

MALIC ACID
Very widespread acid found in apples, grapes and is even the main acid of rhubarb stems.

MALOLACTIC FERMENTATION
Conversion of malic acid to the softer, mellower lactic

acid.

MATURATION

The aging of a wine.

MOUSINESS

A flavour detected mainly on the farwell similar to the smell of mice.

MUST

The liquid and fruit from which the wine is made.

MUSTINESS

A mouldy taste due to leaving the wine standing too long on the lees.

OXIDATION

Any chemical process in which compounds react with the oxygen of the air.

PECTIC ENZYME (PECTOLASE)

An enzyme which breaks down pectin, stopping it from stabilising suspensions in the wine.

PECTIN

Natural 'cement' found between the cells of many fruits. Liberated by boiling and in other ways. If allowed to remain in the wine it will cause a haze. Its presence also reduces the efficiency of the extraction of the fruit juices.

PROOF

An old standard of quoting the alcoholic strength of wines. 100% proof is equal to 57.1 per cent alcohol.

PUNT

Large indentation in the base of the bottle.

RACKING

Separation of the wine from the lees by syphoning.

REDUCTION

Any process by which oxygen is lost from a compound; the reverse of oxidation.

ROSÉ

A delicate pink table wine, usually medium sweet.

SECONDARY FERMENTATION

The anaerobic fermentation, the steady state where new yeast cells are only produced to take the place of those that die. It is during this stage that the maximum conversion of sugar to alcohol occurs.

SOCIAL WINES

Wines designed for drinking unaccompanied by food, they are midway between a dessert and table wine in character.

SODIUM METABISULPHITE

Compound that liberates sulphur dioxide on reaction with an acid.

STARCH

A non-fermentable carbohydrate, which on boiling is converted to a form which will cause a haze in wine.

STARCH ENZYME

Another name for amylase.

STERILISATION

The killing of micro-organisms.

STUCK FERMENT

Premature cessation of fermentation.

SUCROSE

The chemical name for ordinary household sugar.

SULPHITE

Contraction of sodium metabisulphite for which it is used as an abbreviation. Also used to describe the taste of sulphur dioxide dissolved in wine.

SULPHUR DIOXIDE (SO_2)

The gas released by campden tablets or sodium metabisulphite. It is a sterilant and protector of the colour of the wine.

TABLE WINE
The lightest of all wines designed to be drunk with meals.

TANNIN
Compound found in the skins and stems of fruit that leaves a harsh taste on the cheeks and gums.

TARTARIC ACID
Another widespread organic acid, an important component of grape juice.

TAWNY
A rich brown colouration invariably accompanied by an oxidised or maderised taste. Can be an asset in rich dessert wines and sherry style wines, a serious fault in lighter wines.

THIN
A wine lacking in body.

TITRATION
A method of determining the quantity of acid in a wine must by neutralising with sodium hydroxide solution in the presence of an indicator.

VINEGAR
A wine in which some or all of the wine has been converted by micro organisms into acetic acid.

VINOSITY
Wine like character of the liquid.

WOODINESS
A taste resulting from fermenting Prunus fruits in the presence of their stones or blackberries in the presence of their pips.

YEAST
A fungus which converts sugar into alcohol.

INDEX

Tartaric Acid 22
Tawny Wine 134
TCP (Trichlorophenol) 103
Tea 21
Temperature 35, 38, 40, 83
Thiamin 37
Turnips 65

Vanilla 87
Vermouth 66, 158
Vegetable Wine 154
Vinegar 27, 96
Vinegar Fly 97
Vinegar, Mother of 96
Vinosity 17
Vitamins 37

White Currants 59, 126
Wine Press 66
Wormwood 66
Woodiness 104

Yeast 32, 40, 70
Yeast Starter 37, 71
Yeast (harmful) 93, 98
Yeast (wild) 98, 99

NOTES